DATE DUE

JUL 4 2003		
GAYLORD		PRINTED IN U.S.A.

Diversity
Within the Homeless Population:
Implications for Intervention

The *Prevention & Intervention in the Community* series: *
(formerly the *Prevention in Human Services* series)

For information on previous issues of *Prevention in Human Services*, edited by Robert E. Hess please contact: The Haworth Press, Inc., 10 Alice Street, Binghamton, NY 13904-1580 USA.

Diversity
Within the Homeless Population:
Implications for Intervention

Elizabeth M. Smith
Joseph R. Ferrari
Editors

The Haworth Press, Inc.
New York · London

Diversity Within the Homeless Population: Implications for Intervention has also been published as *Journal of Prevention & Intervention in the Community*, Volume 15, Number 2 1997.

Cover design by Thomas J. Mayshock, Jr.

The Haworth Press, Inc., 10 Alice Street, Binghamton, NY 13904-1580 USA

Library of Congress Cataloging-in-Publication Data

Diversity within the homeless population : implications for intervention / Elizabeth M. Smith, Joseph R. Ferrari, editors.
    p. cm.
    Includes bibliographical references and index.
    ISBN 0-7890-0035-0 (alk. paper)
    1. Homeless persons–United States.   2. Social work with the homeless–United States.   I. Smith, Elizabeth M., 1940–.   II. Ferrari, Joseph R.
HV4505.D58 1997   97-5223
362.5′8′0973–dc21   CIP

INDEXING & ABSTRACTING

Contributions to this publication are selectively indexed or abstracted in print, electronic, online, or CD-ROM version(s) of the reference tools and information services listed below. This list is current as of the copyright date of this publication. See the end of this section for additional notes.

- *Abstracts of Research in Pastoral Care & Counseling*, Loyola College, 7135 Minstrel Way, Suite 101, Columbia, MD 21045
- *Behavioral Medicine Abstracts*, University of Washington, School of Social Work, Seattle, WA 98195
- *Child Development Abstracts & Bibliography*, University of Kansas, 2 Bailey Hall, Lawrence, KS 66045
- *CNPIEC Reference Guide: Chinese Directory of Foreign Periodicals*, P.O. Box 88, Beijing, Peoples Republic of China
- *Excerpta Medica/Secondary Publishing Division*, Elsevier Science Inc., Secondary Publishing Division, 655 Avenue of the Americas, New York, NY 10010
- *Family Studies Database (online and CD/ROM)*, National Information Services Corporation, 306 East Baltimore Pike, 2nd Floor, Media, PA 19063
- *IBZ International Bibliography of Periodical Literature*, Zeller Verlag GmbH & Co., P.O.B. 1949, d-49009 Osnabruck, Germany
- *INTERNET ACCESS (& additional networks) Bulletin Board for Libraries ("BUBL"), coverage of information resources on INTERNET, JANET, and other networks.*
  - JANET X.29:UK.AC.BATH.BUBL or 00006012101300
  - TELNET: BUBL.BATH.AC.UK or 138.38.32.45 login 'bubl'
  - Gopher: BUBL.BATH.AC.UK (138.32.32.45). Port 7070
  - World Wide Web: http: // www.bubl.bath.ac.uk./BUBL/ home.html
  - NISSWAIS: telnetniss.ac.uk (for the NISS gateway)
  The Andersonian Library, Curran Building, 101 St. James Road, Glasgow G4 ONS, Scotland
- *Mental Health Abstracts (online through DIALOG)*, IFI/Plenum Data Company, 3202 Kirkwood Highway, Wilmington, DE 19808
- *National Clearinghouse on Child Abuse & Neglect*, 10530 Rosehaven Street, Suite 400, Fairfax, VA 22030-2804
- *NIAAA Alcohol and Alcohol Problems Science Database (ETOH)*, National Institute on Alcohol Abuse and Alcoholism, 1400 Eye Street NW, Suite 600, Washington, DC 20005
- *OT BibSys*, American Occupational Therapy Foundation, P.O. Box 31220, Bethesda, MD 20824-1220

(continued)

- *Referativnyi Zhurnal (Abstracts Journal of the Institute of Scientific Information of the Republic of Russia)*, The Institute of Scientific Information, Baltijskaja ul., 14, Moscow A-219, Republic of Russia

- *RMDB DATABASE (Reliance Medical Information)*, Reliance Medical Information, Inc. (RMI), 100 Putnam Green, Greenwich, CT 06830

- *Social Planning/Policy & Development Abstracts (SOPODA)*, Sociological Abstracts, Inc., P. O. Box 22206, San Diego, CA 92192-0206

- *Social Work Abstracts*, National Association of Social Workers, 750 First Street NW, 8th Floor, Washington, DC 20002

- *Sociological Abstracts (SA)*, Sociological Abstracts, Inc., P. O. Box 22206, San Diego, CA 92192-0206

- *SOMED (social medicine) Database*, Landes Institut fur Den Offentlichen Gesundheitsdienst NRW, Postfach 20 10 12, D-33548 Bielefeld, Germany

- *Violence and Abuse Abstracts: A Review of Current Literature on Interpersonal Violence (VAA)*, Sage Publications, Inc., 2455 Teller Road, Newbury Park, CA 91320

SPECIAL BIBLIOGRAPHIC NOTES

*related to special journal issues (separates)
and indexing/abstracting*

❑ indexing/abstracting services in this list will also cover material in any "separate" that is co-published simultaneously with Haworth's special thematic journal issue or DocuSerial. Indexing/abstracting usually covers material at the article/chapter level.

❑ monographic co-editions are intended for either non-subscribers or libraries which intend to purchase a second copy for their circulating collections.

❑ monographic co-editions are reported to all jobbers/wholesalers/approval plans. The source journal is listed as the "series" to assist the prevention of duplicate purchasing in the same manner utilized for books-in-series.

❑ to facilitate user/access services all indexing/abstracting services are encouraged to utilize the co-indexing entry note indicated at the bottom of the first page of each article/chapter/contribution.

❑ this is intended to assist a library user of any reference tool (whether print, electronic, online, or CD-ROM) to locate the monographic version if the library has purchased this version but not a subscription to the source journal.

❑ individual articles/chapters in any Haworth publication are also available through the Haworth Document Delivery Services (HDDS).

Diversity
Within the Homeless Population:
Implications for Intervention

ABOUT THE EDITORS

Elizabeth M. Smith, PhD, is Associate Professor of Psychiatry in the School of Medicine and Adjunct Associate Professor in the George Warren Brown School of Social Work at Washington University, St. Louis, Missouri. Dr. Smith has conducted numerous research projects, supported by government grants, on homeless women and their children, substance abuse and homelessness, the psychosocial consequences of disaster, and the impact of disaster on children. She has presented papers on disaster and traumatic stress, homelessness, and alcoholic women in lecture series and invitational workshop conferences sponsored by the National Institute of Mental Health and the Missouri Institute of Psychiatry. Her published work appears in journals such as the *American Journal of Psychiatry*, the *Journal of Applied Social Psychology*, and the *Journal of the Addictions*. A member of the Academy of Certified Social Workers, Dr. Smith is an active member of the National Association of Social Workers and of the American Public Health Association.

Joseph R. Ferrari, PhD, is Visiting Assistant Professor in the Department of Psychology at DePaul University in Chicago, Illinois. The Editor-in-Chief of *Journal of Prevention & Intervention in the Community*, he is the author of three books and more than 55 research articles. Dr. Ferrari received his PhD from Adelphi University, with a concentration in experimental social-personality psychology. In addition to his interest in mainstream social psychological issues, such as persuasion, attribution theory, and altruism, he has developed several lines of research in social-community psychology. He is a member of the American Psychological Association, and Fellow in the American Psychological Society. He also is a member of the Society for Community Research and Action.

In Memoriam

Elizabeth M. Smith

Earlier this year, Dr. Elizabeth Smith passed away from cancer. She was a prolific writer, outstanding scientist, wonderful mentor, and distinguished educator. Moreover, to me she was a wonderful friend and colleague. I first had contact with Liz about three years ago when I was helping to develop a federal grant proposal that required tracking "dropouts" from our study. A list of researchers with high success rates in this area was suggested to me, including Elizabeth Smith. I phoned a number of these referrals, and she was the most open and interested of the persons contacted in the project. We then began a series of phone conversations, often talking about other professional issues. Our friendship grew, and in 1995 I invited her to be a member of a panel presentation at the *Midwestern Psychological Association* to present some of our joint research efforts. Unfortunately, her health prevented her from attending, but we met in person another time, here in Chicago, when she visited for a different conference. Her warmth, empathy, and insights were readily apparent at that meeting.

About 18 months ago we discussed editing this volume on "Homelessness." Liz took the lead in contacting colleagues and pulling together the papers you find enclosed. During this period, her illness progressed—unknown to myself, and others. After the volume was finished, sent to the printer, and the galleys reviewed, Liz and I did not have contact for awhile. A couple of phone messages were left, and a few letters sent, but I never had a chance to talk directly with her. I never had the chance to say "bye." There is a definite loss to our profession for her passing, but there is a large personal loss in my life. I will miss my friend.

This volume is dedicated to her memory and her commitment to improving the quality of life for others. Making a difference for others was the goal of her personal and professional life—she'd have it no other way. I hope that readers of this volume become empowered and excited about developing effective programs for the homeless—it is the way she would have wanted it.

Joseph R. Ferrari, PhD

Diversity
Within the Homeless Population:
Implications for Intervention

CONTENTS

ALL HAWORTH BOOKS AND JOURNALS
ARE PRINTED ON CERTIFIED
ACID-FREE PAPER

Social and Environmental Predictors of Adjustment in Homeless Children

Julie M. Passero Rabideau

State University of New York at Buffalo

Paul A. Toro

Wayne State University

(Diversity)

Increasing attention has focused on the fastest growing segment of the homeless population: Children and families. Recent estimates suggest that 500,000 to 1,000,000 children are homeless nationwide (Rosenman & Stein, 1990). It has been estimated that 35% of homeless people are families (mostly women with their children) and that the numbers of homeless families are increasing by rates of 20-30% per year (Waxman & Reyes, 1987). Homeless children have been found to be at risk for a variety of health problems (Wright, 1990) as well as educational delays, poor school

Address correspondence to: Paul A. Toro, Department of Psychology, Wayne State University, 71 West Warren Avenue, Detroit, MI 48202.

The authors wish to thank Charles Bellavia, Diane Cleversley, Chester Daeschler, Stanley Kwilos, Barbara Murie, Sheila Smith, Douglas Snowberger, David Thomas and others associated with the Research Group on Homelessness and Poverty for their help with participant recruitment, data collection, and data analysis. The authors also wish to thank the homeless mothers and children who participated in this research. Finally, the authors thank Murray Levine and Roger V. Burton for comments on an earlier draft of this manuscript.

Funding for this research came from U.S. Department of Labor grant 99-0-3582-79-024-02.

[Haworth co-indexing entry note]: "Social and Enviromental Predictors of Adjustment in Homeless Children." Rabideau, Julie M. Passero, and Paul A. Toro. Co-published simultaneously in *Journal of Prevention & Intervention in the Community* (The Haworth Press, Inc.) Vol. 15, No. 2, 1997, pp. 1-17; and: *Diversity Within the Homeless Population: Implications for Intervention* (ed: Elizabeth M. Smith, and Joseph R. Ferrari) The Haworth Press, Inc., 1997, pp. 1-17. Single or multiple copies of this article are available for a fee from The Haworth Document Delivery Service [1-800-342-9678, 9:00 a.m. - 5:00 p.m. (EST). E-mail address: getinfo@haworth.com].

1

performance, and limited socialization due to poor school attendance (Fox & Roth, 1989). Stigmatization by peers is also common (Gewirtzman & Fodor, 1987). Homeless children also show delayed social and emotional development, including such problems as aggression, withdrawal, social rejection, anxiety, depression, sleep disorders, and abnormal social fears (Bassuk & Rosenberg, 1990; Molnar, Rath, & Klein, 1990; Rafferty & Shinn, 1991).

Though most studies have concluded that homeless children show an increased risk for a range of problems, few have utilized comparison groups of stably-housed poor children in order to differentiate the effects of homelessness from poverty. Studies that have matched homeless children to poor, housed children (typically welfare recipients) have generally found few differences, though both groups differed from the general population on behavior problems and depression (Rafferty & Shinn, 1991). Other studies have found marginally significant differences between homeless and housed comparison groups (e.g., Rescorla et al., 1991). Regardless of whether or not homeless children are worse off than poor housed children, it is clear that many suffer from a range of serious problems. However, there has been little research investigating the risk factors that may lead to greater maladaptation or, alternately, the protective factors that may be related to resilience in the face of adverse and unstable living conditions.

One important risk factor for children in general, and homeless children in particular, may be parental psychopathology. It has been suggested that the effects of homelessness on children's psychological well-being may be mediated by the distress experienced by parents and the resulting disruption this distress has on parenting behaviors (Rafferty & Shinn, 1991). While it has been suggested that mental illness can cause homelessness, it has also been argued that the stresses associated with being homeless may produce emotional disorder (Goodman, Saxe, & Harvey, 1991). Whether parental psychopathology or distress is a cause or an effect of homelessness, it is likely that distress among parents could affect the well-being of their children. Many studies involving nonhomeless populations have found that mothers' psychological functioning is related to symptoms and dysfunction in their children (e.g., Dodge, 1990; Turner, Beidel, & Costello, 1987; Whitbeck et al., 1992).

Stress and social support are two factors which have been studied a great deal in relation to homelessness (Shinn, Knickman, & Weitzman, 1991). The occurrence of acute life events such as eviction, chronic life events such as living in poverty, and chronic, annoying hassles, such as those involved in parenting young children, are common in the lives of homeless women (Milburn & D'Ercole, 1991). Minor parenting hassles have been found to be an important source of stress and contribute to major life stress predictions (Crnic & Greenberg, 1990). The cumulative effect of these various sources of stress serve as a risk factor for homeless mothers by potentially decreasing coping abilities and increasing the likelihood of psychological distress. Social support has been studied as a mediator of stress for homeless women. If social support is effective, it should serve to buffer an individual from the negative effects of stressful life experiences. It has been suggested that adequate social support (be it tangible or emotional) can help women avoid or escape homelessness (Milburn & D'Ercole, 1991). If social support is useful for mothers in reducing stress and alleviating homelessness, social support may serve as a protective factor for children as well, because mothers should be less affected by the stresses they experience and more able to cope with their life circumstances and may be able to escape homelessness more quickly.

Witnessing domestic violence has been consistently found to relate to a variety of poor outcomes in children (Jaffe, Wolfe, & Wilson, 1990). A number of recent studies have found rates of domestic violence to be higher among the homeless than comparable housed persons (e.g., Bassuk & Rosenberg, 1990; Shinn et al., 1991; Toro et al., 1995). Homeless children may often witness such violence and be victimized themselves. Like maltreated children and those from conflictual homes (Grych & Fincham, 1990), more acting-out and other problem behaviors might be expected in homeless children. Furthermore, domestic violence represents one more source of stress in the lives of homeless mothers, and the effects of this stress may very well reduce the mothers' availability for effective parenting and lead to psychological and behavioral problems in their children. Various indicators of poverty have also been consistently found to relate to poor developmental outcomes (Huston, McLoyd, & Garcia Coll, 1994). While all homeless families are poor, they do vary on some key indicators such as levels of income support and the quality of the housing they experienced prior to their episodes of homelessness. Since the quality of shelters for homeless families also varies considerably, the housing environments the children experience during their homelessness also might relate to their outcomes.

METHOD

Sampling and Procedure. The sample included 32 mothers and 68 of their children who were referred through various community agencies and self-referral to the Demonstration Employment Project–Training and

Housing (DEPTH) which was based in Buffalo, New York (metropolitan population of 1 million). DEPTH took an holistic approach that combined services concerned with job training/placement and locating permanent housing and support services, all targeted to the individual's specific needs and oriented toward the long-term goal of helping the person escape homelessness. Central to DEPTH's services was intensive case management, offering access and linkage to services (for further details on the DEPTH program and its evaluation, see Toro et al., 1996). Participants were drawn from a larger sample ($N = 233$) of homeless adults who were referred to the DEPTH program between June and November of 1990 and who received a baseline interview (prior to receiving any intervention services). The data for the present study come entirely from this baseline assessment. Though most participants were homeless at referral, a small number included were in "imminent danger" of becoming homeless. All mothers in the larger DEPTH sample who had children two years of age or older with them were included. Interviews generally lasted 3-4 hours. Because some participants were illiterate, interviewers verbally administered measures to all. The children were interviewed after their mothers, who were typically present during the child's interview. Questions were also read to the children since most did not have adequate reading skills. Some children were not present at the time of their mother's interview, producing missing data on child-rated measures. Adult participants were paid twenty dollars for the time spent in the interview.

Measures: Socioenvironmental and Maternal Characteristics

Stress and Hassles. The Parenting Daily Hassles (PDH) is a 20-item parent-report measure which assesses the frequency and intensity of typical minor but potentially stressful events that tend to occur in families with young children (Crnic & Greenberg, 1990). Both the frequency and intensity scales have acceptable reliability (Chronbach's alpha = .81 and .90, respectively). A total hassles score was constructed by summing the cross-product of frequency $\times$ intensity across all 20 items. The frequency of stressful life events was assessed using an 88-item version of the Social Readjustment Rating Scale (SRRS) which was modified for use with the homeless (Toro et al., 1996). The total number of events that the participant experienced in the previous six months was used. The test-retest reliability of this score, based on a measure similar to that used in the present study, was .84 (Wolfe & Toro, 1992).

Housing, Income, and Services Timeline (HIST). The HIST assesses the life history of homeless adults in five major domains: Housing, homelessness, employment, income, and utilization of social services. Three key

HIST variables were used (test-retest correlations from two other samples of poor and homeless adults appear in parentheses; see Toro et al., 1995, 1996): Time homeless (days in the past 6 months; .73), total income (in the past month, from all sources including public assistance; .81), and housing quality (a composite based on the average across six different environmental ratings completed for each housing situation in the past 12 months; such ratings were also completed for any shelters the family may have stayed at while homeless; .81).

Social Support and Violence. The Social Network Interview (SNI) obtains a list of important network members and provides structural variables characterizing the respondent's social network. This study used a Family Index (a composite reflecting family size and frequency of contact) and a Support Index (reflecting the total number of network members providing support, length of time known, and satisfaction with the support received). The SNI has been used with homeless populations (e.g., Toro et al., 1995, 1996) and one-week test-retest reliability estimates for the indices used, based on a recent study among homeless young adults (Wolfe & Toro, 1992), were .96 (Family) and .98 (Support). The Conflict Tactics Scales (CTS) were used to assess the extent of violence between the mother and her most recent romantic partner (Straus, 1990). The two main scales are Physical Violence and Verbal Aggression (rated with romantic partners as the perpetrator). Across several studies, internal consistency alphas have ranged from .62 to .88 for these two scales and studies using homeless young adults have found test-retest coefficients of .86 to .96 (Toro et al., 1995; Wolfe & Toro, 1992). The CTS has been widely used to assess aggression in the family and validity data indicate that the CTS scales correlate with several risk factors (e.g., unemployment and heavy drinking; Straus et al., 1980). It has recently been used in samples of poor and homeless women with children (Goodman, 1991).

SCL90R Symptom Checklist. The SCL90R is a 90-item self-report measure in which participants rate the amount of distress they have experienced in the past two weeks (Derogatis, 1977). The measure yields a Global Severity Index (GSI) which has demonstrated acceptable internal consistency, test-retest reliability, and other psychometric properties (Derogatis, 1977; Waskow & Parloff, 1974). A number of previous studies on the homeless have utilized the SCL90R or its various brief forms (e.g., Calsyn & Morse, 1990; Toro et al., 1995, 1996; Toro & Wall, 1991).

Measures: Child Adjustment

Child Behavior Checklist (CBCL). The CBCL is a parent-report measure of various child behavior problems (Achenbach, 1991, 1992). Parents are asked to rate the frequency of various behaviors in the past year (two months for 2-3-year-olds) on a 3-point scale. The internalizing dimension is comprised of items related to problems such as depression, social withdrawal, and anxiety. The externalizing dimension consists of items related to such difficulties as aggression, hyperactivity, and conduct disorder. Several previous studies of homeless children have utilized the CBCL (e.g., Bassuk & Rubin, 1987; Christopoulos et al., 1987).

Children's Depression Inventory (CDI). The 27-item CDI (Kovacs, 1983) is a widely used self-report measure for assessing depressive symptomatology in children. The CDI has high internal consistency and has been shown to discriminate between clinical and nonclinical groups (Kazdin, 1990). Children between the ages of 6 and 14 were asked to complete this measure. Several previous studies of homeless children have utilized the CDI to assess depression (e.g., Bassuk & Rubin, 1987).

Perceived Competence Scales (PCS). The PCS assess children's self-perceptions of competence and social acceptance (Harter, 1982). The form for younger children (preschool-grade 2) has 24 items and includes four scales: Cognitive competence, physical competence, peer acceptance, and maternal acceptance. The form for older children (ages 8-18) has 36 items and includes four scales: Cognitive competence, physical competence, social competence, and general self-worth. For the present study, a mean social competence index was derived by summing across items on all scales and dividing by the number of total items. The total PCS scale has been found to have reliability in the mid-to-high .80s (Harter & Pike, 1984). Only children aged 4-14 were asked to complete this measure, as many items were considered inappropriate for older adolescents. The PCS has been used in a study on children in a shelter for battered women (Christopoulos et al., 1987).

Data Analyses

Four hierarchical multiple regression analyses were performed in order to examine the extent to which measures of maternal psychological distress, various stressors, income and housing resources, and social support predicted child outcomes. Child outcomes included the CBCL (internalizing and externalizing scales), CDI depression, and PCS total social competence. Maternal psychological distress was entered in the first step of each regression analysis to statistically control for the relationship between maternal and child psychological functioning. In the second step of each analysis, five indicators of socioenvironmental stress were entered: time homeless, SRRS stressful life events, PDH parenting hassles score, and the CTS verbal aggression and physical violence scores. In the third step,

HIST income and housing quality were entered and, in the final step, the SNI family contact and social support indices were entered. Within the second, third, and fourth hierarchical steps, each set of predictors was entered in a stepwise fashion. Thus, the results for any particular predictor reflect its unique contribution to outcome variance, statistically controlling for all variables entered on earlier hierarchical steps as well as any variables already entered from the predictor's own step (Cohen & Cohen, 1975).

For the CBCL internalizing and externalizing variables, there were complete data for these main analyses on 68 children from 32 families. Complete data were available on 24 children from 13 families for the depression measure and 30 children from 16 families for the competence variable. Because families, rather than children, could be considered as the unit of analysis for this study, a second set of four regression analyses was done based on mean scores across all children in each family (15 of the 32 families had 1 child, 7 had 2 children, 3 had 3, 5 had 4, and 2 had 5). If we obtained roughly comparable findings across the two sets of analyses, we decided we would focus on the individual-level analyses because of a desire to maximize statistical power in our small sample (especially on the child-rated outcomes) and because there was variability of outcome among children within families (making a mean family score difficult to interpret in some cases).

RESULTS

Basic Mother and Child Characteristics. The 32 women in the sample ranged in age from 18 to 41 years (Mean age = 29.6, SD = 6.7). Fourteen of the women were white, 14 others were African-American, and four were Hispanic. Most of the 32 women were currently separated or divorced, though 4 were currently married and living with their husbands and 10 had never been married. Almost half of the mothers had only one dependent child with them, 10 had two or three, and 7 others had four or five. Four of the women were not homeless at the time of the interview (the imminently homeless). Most of the remaining women had been homeless in their current episode for three months or less (Mean days homeless was 89.8; SD = 195.8; median = 44 days). All of the four imminently homeless women had experienced homelessness at some earlier point in their lives; in fact, this was not the first instance of homelessness for the majority of the 32 women (Mean total lifetime episodes was 2.6, SD = 2.0). As has been found in other studies comparing women homeless with their children to single women and men (e.g., Roll, Toro, & Ortola, 1995), the women in the present study ($n = 32$) differed from the remainder of the mostly male (70.5%) DEPTH sample ($n = 193$ with complete data) in that they were more likely to be currently married or have been previously married (68.8% of the mothers vs. 42.9% of the remaining DEPTH sample; $\chi^2(1) = 7.34$, $p < .01$), more likely to have received public assistance in the past year (87.5% of the mothers vs. 54.4% of the remaining sample; $\chi^2(1) = 12.36$, $p < .01$), and less likely to have worked in the past year (21.9% of the mothers vs. 73.1% of the remaining sample; $\chi^2(1) = 31.54$, $p < .01$). The mothers also reported higher levels of psychological distress on the SCL90R ($M = .95$ vs. .71 for the remaining sample; $F(1,223) = 4.25$, $p < .05$) and more family contact ($M = .72$ on the SNI Family Index for the mothers vs. $-.09$ for the remaining sample; $F(1,220) = 7.03$, $p < .01$).

The sample included 42 males and 26 females and was quite young (mean age = 6.0, SD = 3.7). Thirty-five were preschoolers (ages 2-5), 25 were school-aged children (ages 6-11), and eight were adolescents (ages 12-15). These and most other characteristics of the sample are generally consistent with the samples in other studies of homeless families (e.g., Bassuk & Rubin, 1987; Boxill & Beaty, 1990; Burt & Cohen, 1989). The young age of the children in this and other samples may be a function of the policy of some shelters not to allow children over a certain age. Though, compared to some existing studies of homeless families (e.g., Burt & Cohen, 1989; Shinn et al., 1991), our sample included a somewhat larger proportion of whites, the ethnic breakdown was similar to that observed in the remainder of the DEPTH sample ($N = 193$), to samples in prior studies done in Buffalo (e.g., Toro et al., 1995, 1996; Toro & Wall, 1991), and to samples of homeless families in some prior studies (e.g., Goodman, 1991).

Descriptive Findings on Child Adjustment. Many of the children were experiencing considerable adjustment difficulties. The scores for the group of 68 children on the Internalizing (mean = 54.7) and Externalizing (mean = 55.5) scales of the CBCL were higher than those of a normed community sample by about one-half of a standard deviation in each case. By maternal report, six (8.8%) of these children exhibited a level of behavioral disturbance for the internalizing dimension that suggests the need for mental health services, while eight (11.8%) had scores in this range for the externalizing dimension (see Achenbach, 1991, 1992). Twenty-four of the 32 children aged 6 to 14 (75.0%) completed the CDI. Although the mothers reported a relatively small percentage of internalizing behavior problems, the mean CDI score for these children was 11.3. Fourteen (58.3%) scored above a score of nine which indicates the need for a mental health evaluation (see Kovacs, 1983; Kovacs & Beck, 1977). Rafferty and Shinn (1991) describe several studies of homeless children that have found 50-54% in need of mental health services based on this CDI cutoff score of nine. Of the 44 children aged four to 14, 30 (68.2%) completed the PCS. While some of the children who did not complete this measure were not present during their mothers' interviews, some younger children failed to complete this measure because they could not adequately conceptualize the task. The mean score for the group was 3.2 (standard deviation = 0.5). This mean score is consistent with those found in norming samples of preschool and elementary-aged children (see Harter, 1982; Harter & Pike, 1984). Thus, these children's self-perceptions of social competence are generally positive and comparable to the general population.

Predictors of Child Adjustment. All four final regression equations on the total sample of children (maximum $N = 68$), each including a total of 10 predictors, were statistically significant ($p < .05$; see Tables 1 and 2). In the first of these analyses, the level of parenting daily hassles reported by the mothers (after controlling for maternal distress, time homeless, and stressful life events) was significantly related to higher levels of internalizing behavior problems in their children. More verbal aggression in the mothers' romantic relationships (after controlling for maternal distress, time homeless, stressful life events, and parenting hassles) was also significantly related to higher levels of internalizing behavior problems. In the second analysis, higher parenting daily hassles was significantly related to higher levels of externalizing behavior problems in the children. More physical violence in the mothers' recent romantic relationships, poorer housing quality, and more family contact were also significantly related to higher levels of externalizing behavior problems. In this analysis, the family contact index yielded a complex suppression effect (note the different signs of the simple bivariate r and the β in Table 1; see Cohen & Cohen, 1975). Post-hoc regression analyses done to elucidate the nature of this suppression effect suggested that family contact, on a simple bivariate level, may have a positive influence on child outcome. However, if one removes the effects of the suppressor variables (all of which overlap with the family index) from externalizing problems, a "bad side" of family contact emerges.

In the third multiple regression analysis, more physical violence in the mothers' romantic relationships was related to higher child self-ratings of depression. In addition, a greater level of social support reported within the mother's social network was significantly related to lower child-rated depression. In the final analysis, more maternal psychological distress was significantly related to lower child-rated social competence. Higher total

TABLE 1. Two hierarchical regression analyses on mother-rated adjustment variables.

Criterion	Simple	Individual Predictors			Overall Equation	
Predictor	r	β	sr^2	F	R^2	F
Internalizing Problems					.356	3.15**
Maternal Distress	−.12	−.12	.014	.96		
Time Homeless	.07	−.04	.001	.13		
Life Events	.15	.13	.014	1.17		
Parenting Hassles	.34**	.37	.130	9.80**		
Verbal Aggression	.28*	.32	.098	8.35**		
Physical Violence	.19	−.09	.004	.30		
Total Income	−.05	−.11	.010	.78		
Housing Quality	−.12	−.06	.002	.20		
Family Index	−.04	.32	.038	3.19		
Support Index	−.03	−.25	.045	3.95		
Externalizing Problems					.474	5.13**
Maternal Distress	−.18	−.18	.032	2.15		
Time Homeless	.24	.10	.008	.82		
Life Events	.12	.16	.022	2.11		
Parenting Hassles	.43**	.47	.218	18.89**		
Verbal Aggression	.19	−.00	.000	.00		
Physical Violence	.27*	.28	.078	7.47**		
Total Income	−.02	−.07	.003	.36		
Housing Quality	−.30*	−.24	.041	4.01*		
Family Index	−.25*	.33	.042	4.37*		
Support Index	−.05	−.20	.030	3.22		

Note. $N = 68$ for all statistics presented in this table.
*$p < .05$ **$p < .01$

income and social support reported by the mother also predicted higher child-rated social competence.

Across all four main analyses, two of the ten predictors (length of time homeless and total stressful life events) failed to significantly contribute to the prediction of child adjustment. In addition, the magnitude of the significant relationships obtained was generally modest, with significant predictors usually accounting for less than 20% of the unique variance in adjustment variables (based on sr^2 and controlling for variables entered earlier in the hierarchical regression analyses). However, in four cases, the amount

TABLE 2. Two hierarchical regression analyses on child-rated adjustment variables.

Criterion	Simple	Individual Predictors			Overall Equation	
Predictor	r	β	sr²	F	R²	F
Depression[a]			.674	4.12*		
Maternal Distress	.15	.13	.022	.50		
Time Homeless	.01	.02	.000	.00		
Life Events	.17	.09	.007	.22		
Parenting Hassles	.35	.36	.103	2.46		
Verbal Aggression	.18	.07	.002	.04		
Physical Violence	.31	.55	.202	6.00*		
Total Income	−.17	.39	.038	.96		
Housing Quality	.11	.29	.012	.31		
Family Index	−.11	.53	.022	1.26		
Support Index	−.49*	−.87	.364	20.41**		
Social Competence[b]			.575	2.57*		
Maternal Distress	−.46	−.41	.210	7.43*		
Time Homeless	.12	.01	.001	.01		
Life Events	−.06	.11	.012	.42		
Parenting Hassles	−.37*	−.27	.057	2.10		
Verbal Aggression	.05	.05	.001	.04		
Physical Violence	−.07	−.10	.008	.31		
Total Income	.58**	.60	.155	6.15*		
Housing Quality	.16	.11	.005	.19		
Family Index	.04	−.16	.006	.25		
Support Index	.54**	.52	.120	5.57*		

[a]$N = 24$ [b]$N = 30$
*$p < .05$ **$p < .01$

of variance accounted for was 20% or more: Parenting hassles as a predictor of externalizing problems (22%), physical violence and the support index predicting child depression (20% and 36%, respectively), and maternal distress as a predictor of child social competence (21%). Finally, the pattern of results from the second set of four regression analyses (based on mean scores across all children in each family, $N = 32$) was similar to that based on individual children as the unit of analysis. Therefore, in the discussion below, we will focus on the individual-level analyses.

DISCUSSION

Consistent with other studies of homeless children that have used the CDI and CBCL, this study found the children were experiencing more behavior problems and depression as compared to community norms (Bassuk & Rosenberg, 1990; Bassuk & Rubin, 1987; Rescorla, Parker, & Stolley, 1991). Based on maternal report, six times as many children as expected were exhibiting externalizing behavior problems that indicated the need for mental health services and four times more were exhibiting internalizing behavior problems. The lack of routine and supervision associated with being homeless could contribute to the particularly high level of externalizing behavior. Of those children completing the CDI, over half scored above the cutoff indicating the need for mental health services. Homeless children have many needs, not the least of which are ones in the mental health domain. On the positive side, the homeless children in our sample generally reported social competence in the normative range. This finding points out that homeless children do not uniformly show deficits on all dimensions. On the contrary, they may have certain strengths that can be maximized to assist their future adjustment. Workers may want to attend to such strengths, as well as the obvious problems, when designing interventions for homeless children.

In the main analyses identifying the social and environmental predictors of child outcomes, several variables showed a pattern of relationships (i.e., significant results in more than one of the four regression analyses done). The extent of domestic violence in the mother's most recent romantic relationships yielded significant results in three of four analyses. When the mother reported greater physical violence from her partner, the child tended to report greater depression and the mother rated more externalizing problems in the child. When the mother reported greater verbal aggression from her partner, she also rated more internalizing problems in the child. The greater degree of externalizing problems in these homeless children can be explained by modeling: The children see violence and imitate it. As suggested in the literature review, this finding could also reflect the effects of domestic violence on the mother: The particular stresses associated with such violence may make the mother especially unavailable for consistent parenting, resulting in uncontrollable behavior on the part of the child. It is interesting that domestic violence was even more strongly related to internalizing behaviors of the child (including self-rated depression). The sense of helplessness that the mother may experience as a function of violence may engender a particularly pernicious sense of confusion and a similar helplessness on the part of the child. In addition, it is possible that the child may also be a victim at the hands of the mother's violent partners (often unrelated boyfriends). Future studies may want to assess violence against the child as well as that against the child's primary caretaker.

The level of parenting hassles related both to internalizing and externalizing behavior problems in the children. An obvious explanation here is that homeless mothers (like non-homeless mothers) with children who have behavior problems, for whatever reason, are bound to encounter additional hassles in coping with such children. However, it is also possible that mothers who perceive high levels of parenting stress may view their children's behaviors more negatively. Given the correlational nature of the study's findings, either interpretation is plausible. The amount and quality of social support that the mothers received emerged as an important factor predicting how children feel about themselves. This predictor was related to both child-rated depression and perceived social competence. These effects were found even after controlling for all eight other predictors which were entered on earlier steps in each hierarchical analysis. This suggests that the help a mother receives benefits not only her directly, but benefits her children as well; in other words, maternal social support may serve as a protective factor that facilitates resiliency in homeless children. For multi-problem families, such as those who are homeless, interventions at the family level may often be appropriate. Some intervention strategies for assisting homeless families involve the reestablishment or enhancement of existing social networks (Hutchison, Searight, & Stretch, 1986). Based on these results, it may be useful to further investigate this area to determine which aspects of maternal social support are most useful for promoting children's positive socioemotional functioning, and target these interventions in ways to maximize the benefit to children. It may also be useful to directly assess children's perceptions of their own and their families' social support in order to determine what children perceive as most helpful.

It is unclear why the predicted relationship between maternal psychological distress and maternal-reported child behavior problems was generally not present. Only in the analysis involving child-rated competence was the predicted relationship found. It is possible that mothers who are preoccupied with their own distress do not notice as many behavior problems in their children. Supporting this theory, there were small, negative correlations between maternal psychological distress and maternal report of both internalizing and externalizing behavior problems ($rs = -.12$ and $-.18$, respectively), suggesting a slight trend for mothers experiencing increased distress of their own to report fewer behavior problems in their children. Another explanation for this general lack of findings involves the fact that, for children, homelessness results in disruptions in multiple areas, including home life, school attendance, contact with friends, and, possibly, contact with relatives, and requires the major readjustment to a shelter or other living situation. The contribution of maternal distress to the development of depression and other symptoms in homeless children may be negligible as compared to the impact of all of the other changes that these children are experiencing. Finally, it is possible that the SCL90R, which measured the level of distress experienced in the past two weeks, does not reflect long-standing psychopathology per se in these homeless mothers but, rather, may represent a transient reaction to a set of stressful circumstances.

Two variables failed to predict child outcomes in any of the analyses: The total time the family was homeless during the past 6 months and total stressful life events (as experienced by the mother in the past 6 months). These variables were not as potent as expected, while several other variables had a greater impact on the outcomes experienced by homeless children. In a few cases it also appeared that maternal distress, which was entered in each analysis prior to these two variables, diminished the modest bivariate relationships these variables had with the outcome.

Several important limitations of this study should be noted. Because the data collected were correlational in nature, it is impossible to establish the causal direction of the effects found. Prospective studies of homeless children are needed to better explore causal linkages. The sample size, especially for analyses involving the depression and competence measures, was small. As a result, the findings must be viewed with caution and replicated with larger samples. Additionally, this sample of children was not randomly collected but, rather, represented the children "attached" to adults referred to a community agency. Thus, it is not clear how well these children represent the total population of homeless children. Furthermore, the children in this study were living in a variety of situations: Some were in shelters, some lived doubled up with relatives or friends of their mothers. A small number were not, in fact, homeless at the time of interview but, rather, were in imminent danger of becoming homeless (e.g., about to be evicted). Most other studies on homeless children have only sampled in shelters. This reduces the ability to compare this study to these others, although most basic sample characteristics were similar to prior samples. On the flip side of this disadvantage, however, is an advantage of this study: A wider range of homeless children was studied, so that, in some respects, this sample may be more representative than previous studies of homeless children. As a final limitation, no comparison group of poor children at no immediate risk for homelessness was included. The inclusion of such a comparison group in future research could help determine whether the increased risk for maladaptation in homeless children is a function of homelessness, or alternately, a function of extreme poverty.

Despite these limitations, the findings of this study have a number of implications for intervention. Like Masten (1992, p. 43) we suspect that "multiple strategies at many levels of intervention will be required to improve the odds for good developmental outcomes in these (homeless) children." Based on our findings, such strategies could include parent counseling to help mothers cope with stress, family therapy and conflict resolution to address the prevalent domestic violence experienced by homeless families, financial counseling to improve family income, and the mobilization of existing social support networks to help the mothers re-establish quality housing environments for themselves and their children. Further research will be necessary both to replicate these findings, to discover other protective factors that may lessen the impact of homelessness on children, and to evaluate such intervention strategies.

REFERENCES

Achenbach, T. M. (1991). *Manual for the Child Behavior Checklist/4-18 and 1991 Profile.* Burlington, VT: University of Vermont Department of Psychiatry.

Achenbach, T. M. (1992). *Manual for the Child Behavior Checklist/2-3 and 1992 Profile.* Burlington, VT: University of Vermont Department of Psychiatry.

Bassuk, E. L., & Rosenberg, L. (1990). Psychosocial characteristics of homeless children and children with homes. *Pediatrics, 85,* 257-261.

Bassuk, E. L., & Rubin, L. (1987). Homeless children: A neglected population. *American Journal of Orthopsychiatry, 57,* 279-286.

Boxill, N. A., & Beaty, A. L. (1990). Mother/child interaction among homeless women and their children in a public night shelter in Atlanta, Georgia. *Child & Youth Services, 14,* 49-64.

Burt, M. R., & Cohen, B. E. (1989). Differences among homeless single women, women with children, and single men. *Social Problems, 36,* 508-524.

Calsyn, R. J., & Morse, G. (1990). Homeless men and women: Commonalties and a service gender gap. *American Journal of Community Psychology, 18,* 597-608.

Christopoulos, C., Cohn, D. A., Shaw, D. S., Joyce, S., Sullivan-Hanson, J., Kraft, S. P., & Emery, R. E. (1987). Children of abused women: I. Adjustment at time of shelter residence. *Journal of Marriage and the Family, 49,* 611-619.

Cohen, J., & Cohen, P. (1975). *Applied multiple regression/correlation analysis for the behavioral sciences.* Hillsdale, NJ: Lawrence Erlbaum.

Cohen, S., Marmelstein, R., Kamarch, T., & Hoberman, H. (1985). Measuring the functional components of social support. In I. Sarason & B. Sarason (Eds.),

Social support: Theory, research, and applications. Dordrecht, The Netherlands: Martinus Nijhoff.

Crnic, K. A., & Greenberg, M. T. (1990). Minor parenting stresses with young children. *Child Development, 61,* 1628-1637.

Derogatis, L. R. (1977). SCL-90-R (revised version) Manual I. Baltimore, MD: Johns Hopkins University School of Medicine.

Dodge, K. A. (1990). Developmental psychopathology in children of depressed mothers. *Developmental Psychology, 26,* 3-6.

Fox, E. R., & Roth, L. (1989). Homeless children: Philadelphia as a case study. *Annals of the American Academy of Political and Social Sciences, 506,* 141-151.

Gewirtzman, R., & Fodor, I. (1987). The homeless child at school: From welfare hotel to classroom. *Child Welfare, 66,* 237-245.

Goodman, L. A. (1991). The prevalence of abuse in the lives of homeless and housed poor mothers: A comparison study. *American Journal of Orthopsychiatry, 61,* 489-500.

Goodman, L., Saxe, L., & Harvey, M. (1991). Homelessness as psychological trauma: Broadening perspectives. *American Psychologist, 46,* 1219-1225.

Grych, J. H., & Fincham, F. D. (1990). Marital conflict and children's adjustment: A cognitive-contextual framework. *Psychological Bulletin, 108,* 267-290.

Harter, S. (1982). The perceived competence scale for children. *Child Development, 53,* 87-97.

Harter, S. & Pike, R. (1984). Pictorial scale of perceived competence and social acceptance for young children. *Child Development, 55,* 1969-1982.

Huston, A. C., McLoyd, V. C., & Garcia Coll, C. (1994). Children and poverty: Issues in contemporary research. *Child Development, 65,* 275-282.

Hutchison, W. J., Searight, P., & Stretch, J. J. (1986). Multidimensional networking: A response to the needs of homeless families. *Social Work, 31,* 427-430.

Jaffe, P. G., Wolfe, D. A., & Wilson, S. K. (1990). *Children of battered women.* Newbury Park, CA: Sage.

Kazdin, A. E. (1990). Childhood depression. *Journal of Child Psychology and Psychiatry, 31,* 121-160.

Kovacs, M. (1983). *The Children's Depression Inventory: A self-rated depression scale for school age youngsters.* Pittsburgh, PA: University of Pittsburgh, School of Medicine.

Kovacs, M. & Beck, A. T. (1977). An empirical-clinical approach toward a definition of childhood depression. In J. Schulterbrandt & A. Raskin (Eds.), *Depression in childhood: Diagnosis, treatment, and conceptual models.* New York: Raven Press.

Masten, A. S. (1992). Homeless children in the United States: Mark of a nation at risk. *Current Directions in Psychological Science, 1,* 41-44.

Milburn, N., & D'Ercole, A. (1991). Homeless women: Moving toward a comprehensive model. *American Psychologist, 46,* 1161-1169.

Molnar, J. M., Rath, W. R., & Klein, T. P. (1990). Constantly compromised: The impact of homelessness on children. *Journal of Social Issues, 46*(4), 109-124.

Rafferty, Y., & Shinn, M. (1991). The impact of homelessness on children. *American Psychologist, 46,* 1170-1179.

Rescorla, L., Parker, R., & Stolley, P. (1991). Ability, achievement, and adjustment in homeless children. *American Journal of Orthopsychiatry, 61,* 210-220.

Roll, C.N., Toro, P.A., & Ortola, G.L. (1995). Characteristics and experiences of homeless adults: A comparison of single men and single women and women with children. Presented at the Annual meeting of the American Public Health Association in San Diego, California.

Rosenman, M., & Stein, M. L. (1990). Homeless children: A new vulnerability. *Child & Youth Services, 14,* 89-109.

Shinn, M., Knickman, J. R., & Weitzman, B. C. (1991). Social relationships and vulnerability to becoming homeless among poor families. *American Psychologist, 46,* 1180-1187.

Straus, M. (1990). The Conflict Tactics Scales and its critics: An evaluation and new data on validity and reliability. In M. A. Straus & R. J. Gelles, *Physical violence in American families: Risk factors and adaptations to violence in 8,145 families.* New Brunswick, NJ: Transaction Press.

Straus, M. A., Gelles, R. J., & Steinmetz, S. K. (1980). *Behind closed doors: Violence in the American family.* New York: Doubleday/Anchor.

Toro, P. A., Bellavia, C., Daeschler, C., Owens, B., Wall, D. D., Passero, J. M., & Thomas, D. M. (1995). Distinguishing homelessness from poverty: A comparative study. *Journal of Consulting and Clinical Psychology, 63,* 280-289.

Toro, P. A., Rabideau, J. M. P., Bellavia, C., Daeschler, C., Wall, D. D., Thomas, D. M., & Smith, S. J. (1996, in press). Evaluating an intervention for homeless persons: Results of a field experiment. *Journal of Consulting and Clinical Psychology.*

Toro, P. A., & Wall, D. D. (1991). Research on homeless persons: Diagnostic comparisons and practice implications. *Professional Psychology: Research and Practice, 22,* 479-488.

Turner, S. M., Biedel, D. C., & Costello, A. (1987). Psychopathology in the offspring of anxiety disordered patients. *Journal of Consulting and Clinical Psychology, 55,* 229-235.

Waskow, I., & Parloff, M. (1974). *Psychotherapy change measures.* Washington, DC: Superintendent of Documents, US Government Printing Office.

Waxman, L. D., & Reyes, L. M. (1987, May). *A status report on homeless families in American cities.* Washington: United States Conference of Mayors.

Whitbeck, L. B., Hoyt, D. R., Simons, R. L., Conger, R. D., Elder, G. H., Lorenz, F. O., & Huck, S. (1992). Intergenerational continuity of parental rejection and depressed affect. *Journal of Personality and Social Psychology, 63,* 1036-1045.

Wolfe, S. M., & Toro, P. A. (1992). *People and transitions in housing (PATH) project: Pilot reliability study.* Unpublished report, Department of Psychology, Wayne State University, Detroit, MI.

Wright, J. D. (1990). Homelessness is not healthy for children and other living things. *Child & Youth Services, 14,* 65-88.

Differences in Psychosocial Factors Among Older and Younger Homeless Adolescents Found in Youth Shelters

Lisa M. Boesky
University of Washington

Paul A. Toro
Pamela A. Bukowski
Wayne State University

During the past decade, the problem of homelessness has received increasing attention across the United States (Toro & McDonell, 1992). More young people are becoming homeless and it is estimated that 25% of the homeless population is less than 18 years of age (Hombs, 1990). Studies suggest that 9-15% of adolescents have at some time run away from home or been thrown out by their parents (Ringwalt, Greene, &

Address correspondence to: Paul A. Toro, Department of Psychology, Wayne State University, 71 West Warren Avenue, Detroit, MI 48202.

The authors wish to thank Nyama Reed, Jerry Rogers, Steven Schoeberlein, Virginia Szymanski, Susan Wolfe, and others associated with The Research Group on Homelessness and Poverty for their help with participant recruitment, data collection, and data analysis. The authors also wish to thank the youth shelters and homeless youth who participated in this research.

Funding for this research came from Wayne State University.

[Haworth co-indexing entry note]: "Differences in Psychosocial Factors Among Older and Younger Homeless Adolescents Found in Youth Shelters." Boesky, Lisa M., Paul A. Toro, and Pamela A. Bukowski. Co-published simultaneously in *Journal of Prevention & Intervention in the Community* (The Haworth Press, Inc.) Vol. 15, No. 2, 1997, pp. 19-36; and: *Diversity Within the Homeless Population: Implications for Intervention* (ed: Elizabeth M. Smith, and Joseph R. Ferrari) The Haworth Press, Inc., 1997, pp. 19-36. Single or multiple copies of this article are available for a fee from The Haworth Document Delivery Service [1-800-342-9678, 9:00 a.m. - 5:00 p.m. (EST). E-mail address: getinfo@haworth.com].

Iachan, 1994; Windle, 1989). Although many of these youth will return home within a week, a number of them become recurrent or chronic runaways and homelessness becomes a way of life for them. These homeless adolescents can be exposed to a great deal of dangerous behavior including crime, prostitution, and drug and alcohol abuse.

The current study was conducted with adolescents who spent the previous night in a shelter for homeless youth and were unaccompanied by a parent or legal guardian. Some of these youth have "run away" from home, others have been forced to leave home by their parents ("throwaways"), and still others are temporarily seeking services with the full knowledge of their parents. Some have spent time living on the streets, others have not. Some have experienced long and/or repeated episodes of homelessness, and others are having their first experience with homelessness and/or have been homeless only for a few days. To avoid the sort of terminological confusion common in the existing literature, throughout this paper we will refer to the overall group as "homeless" youth, understanding that the population is heterogeneous.

Despite their numbers, homeless youth are perhaps the least studied group within the overall homeless population and some existing studies have been based largely on subjective impressions rather than on objective empirical information (Robertson, 1991). The homeless youth population is diverse and one must be aware of the differences among subgroups so services can be matched to the adolescent's specific needs and difficulties. Little attention has been given to the relationship between developmental differences and psychosocial factors among homeless youth. Because differences in psychosocial factors have been found among younger and older adolescents in the general population, one might expect such differences among homeless adolescents as well.

The present study had two purposes. First, we attempted to document the characteristics of a large and representative sample of homeless adolescents. Unlike many prior studies, we took an objective empirical approach based on measures with established reliability and validity and assessed many domains, including family environment, social network, psychopathology, and substance abuse. The study also randomly sampled adolescents from the full range of shelters for homeless youth in a major metropolitan area. Samples in past studies have generally been small and gathered from a single site, limiting generalizability. Many past studies have also focused on the relatively small subgroup of street youth who are visible in certain major cities (e.g., Cauce et al., 1994; Robertson, 1990). We chose to focus on the larger group of sheltered youth who exist in virtually every major metropolitan area. We also chose to limit our sample to minors, i.e., those under age 18. Some existing studies have considered persons as old as age 21 as "adolescents" (e.g., Cauce et al., 1994). The study's second purpose was to investigate age differences among homeless adolescents, a topic largely ignored in past studies. Such differences could have implications for policy decisions as well as intervention programs. For example, because it is unknown whether younger and older homeless adolescents are experiencing the same difficulties, it is not clear whether treatment strategies should be designed for a homogenous group or whether older and younger homeless adolescents should be treated differently. Similarly, with regard to prevention programs, it is not known whether the risk factors for homelessness differ across developmental stages.

METHOD

Sample Selection. The study included 122 adolescents between ages 12 and 17 who had spent the previous night at a shelter for homeless youth. The sample was recruited over a full calendar year from all six major homeless youth shelters in the seven-county Detroit metropolitan area (total 1990 population of 4.4 million). Across these shelters and those in other cities, children under age 12 (unaccompanied by parents) are rare. Each of the shelters provided service utilization data and the number sampled from each shelter was proportional to the number of youth served over the prior year. Even though the individual shelters differed somewhat in terms of the clientele they served, our probability sampling technique provided a cross-section of homeless youth. The two largest shelters each had annual caseloads of about 300 adolescents and, together, accounted for more than half (60.7%) of the final sample. One of these shelters served an urban population composed primarily of nonwhites and had a somewhat higher percentage of girls and the other served a largely suburban population that included a somewhat higher percentage of girls, fewer nonwhite youth, and the youngest clientele. Three of the other (smaller) shelters served suburban populations which were mostly white and somewhat older. The final shelter focused on homeless women and girls engaged in prostitution in the downtown area of Detroit. Most of those served by this agency were 18 or over and so were not included in our sample.

Measures

Background, Family, and Other Basic Characteristics. In addition to obtaining demographic information, adolescents were asked why they were currently seeking services at a homeless shelter. Adolescents were classified into one of three categories: (1) runaways, (2) throwaways, and (3) intervention seekers. The runaways left home without parental permission and the throwaway adolescents were forced to leave home. The parents of intervention seekers knew their whereabouts and both they and the youth expected the youth to return home after a brief period. The Inventory of Childhood Events (ICE) was developed to measure perceived childhood experiences and family history (Zozus & Zax, 1989), has been used in various studies of mostly young homeless adults (Rabideau & Toro, 1996; Toro et al., 1995), and has consistently yielded three dimensions in factor analyses: (1) Positive, indicating a family in which there is warmth and caring; (2) Dysfunctional, a family with absent parental figures, substance abuse, and other factors indicating neglect; and (3) Punitive, a family in which punishment and other negative parenting practices are common (an analysis done on the present sample identified the same factors). In addition to the three factor scores, the present study included additional ICE individual items assessing physical and sexual abuse and neglect. The Family Environment Scale (FES) was used to assess the social climate of the homeless adolescent's family of origin (sometimes this was a foster family). Four FES scales were administered: Cohesion, Expressiveness, Conflict, and Independence. There is evidence of sufficient reliability for these four scales, with internal consistency alphas ranging from .61 to .78 when used with homeless young adults (Wolfe & Toro, 1992). Test-retest reliability estimates of .68 to .86 have been reported in normative samples and considerable validity data also exist (Moos & Moos, 1986). The Conflict Tactics Scales (CTS) were used to assess the extent of violence between parent and adolescent (Straus, 1990). The two main scales are Physical Violence and Verbal Aggression. The adolescent was asked to rate the frequency of occurrence of tactics their parents had used toward them when attempting to resolve conflict and also the tactics they used toward their parents. Across several studies, internal consistency alphas have ranged from .62 to .88 for these two scales and reliability studies with homeless young adults have found test-retest coefficients of .86 to .96 (Toro et al., 1995; Wolfe & Toro, 1992). The CTS has been widely used to assess aggression in the family and validity data indicate that the CTS scales correlate with several risk factors (e.g., unemployment and heavy drinking; Straus et al., 1980).

The Housing, Education, and Services Measure (HES), adapted from a similar measure for homeless adults (Toro et al., 1995), obtains a history of housing and homelessness and includes questions regarding mental health, substance abuse, and other social services utilized. The measure has demonstrated adequate reliability with homeless young adults (Wolfe & Toro, 1992). The following variables were used: (a) number of lifetime housing moves; (b) time in out-of-home placements; (c) time spent homeless (in lifetime); and (e) time involved with outpatient psychological services. The Social Network Interview (SNI) obtains a list of important network members and provides structural variables characterizing the respondent's social network. This study used a Family Index (a composite reflecting family size and frequency of contact), a Friend Index (reflecting the number of friends, length of time known, and frequency of contact), and a Support Index (reflecting the total number of network members providing support, length of time known, and satisfaction with the support received). The SNI has been used with homeless populations (e.g., Toro et al. 1995) and one-week test-retest reliability estimates for the indices used, based on a recent study among homeless young adults (Wolfe & Toro, 1992), ranged from .82 (Friend) to .98 (Support).

Psychopathology, Self-Esteem/Efficacy, Stress, and Health. The Diagnostic Interview Schedule for Children–2nd Edition (DISC) is a structured interview that elicits DSM-III-R diagnostic criteria for common forms of psychopathology found in children and adolescents. It was designed to be administered by interviewers without clinical experience following a training period. The following disorders were assessed in this study: Depression, mania, disruptive disorders (attention-deficit disorder, oppositional-defiant disorder, and conduct disorder), alcohol abuse/dependence, and drug abuse/dependence. The DISC documented reliability and validity (Costello, Edelbrock, & Costello, 1985; Shaffer et al., 1993) and has recently been used in a study of homeless youth (Cauce et al., 1994). The Brief Symptom Inventory (BSI), a 53-item version of the SCL90R, provided an additional method to assess psychopathology. The general severity index used provides an overall indication of psychological distress currently experienced by the adolescent. Evidence is available on internal consistency and concurrent and discriminant validity (Derogatis & Melisaratos, 1983). The BSI and other forms of the SCL90R have been used in a number of studies of homeless adults (e.g., Morse & Calsyn, 1986; Toro et al., 1995; Toro & Wall, 1991). The Rosenberg Self-Esteem Scale consists of 10 items originally designed for adolescents (Rosenberg, 1965). It has been shown to have good internal consistency (alpha = .92) and test-retest reliability (rs = .85-.88) and there is considerable research demonstrating construct validity (Corcoran & Fischer, 1987). A total self-esteem score was used. The Self-Efficacy Scale (SES) has 23 items that assess self-efficacy expectations and yields two subscales: (a) General and (b) Social Self-Efficacy. When given to college students, both subscales have demonstrated good reliability (coefficients of .71-.86 for the two scales, respectively). There is also good evidence of construct and predictive validity (Sherer et al., 1982). The Physical Health Checklist (PHC) assesses the number of health symptoms that have bothered the adolescent in the past 6 months. There is evidence of sufficient test-retest reliability ($r = .85$) when used with homeless adults (Wolfe & Toro, 1992). The Modified Life Events Interview (MLEI) was developed for use with homeless populations (Lovell, 1984) and assesses the number of stressful events experienced in the past 6 months. Items reflect a number of life domains including social relationships, housing situations, employment, education/job training, and mental and physical health. The total score has good test-retest reliability ($r = .84$) when used with homeless adults (Wolfe & Toro, 1992).

Procedure. Each youth was randomly selected from among those currently in residence at the shelter. Interviews were conducted by graduate and advanced undergraduate students in psychology. Interviewers were trained in the administration of the interview, as well as practical and safety issues involved in dealing with homeless adolescents, some of whom had personal or emotional problems. A trusted staff member was usually present when the purpose of the study was explained. There were no refusals. The staff member left after the consent process and then each adolescent participant completed a 3-4 hour interview (sometimes it was necessary to conduct the interview over more than one session). All measures were administered verbally by the interviewer, since some of the youth had limited reading ability. Most interviews took place in private rooms at the shelter. Each adolescent was paid five dollars for participation.

In order to examine age differences, nine hierarchical multiple regression analyses were done, with variables of interest as predictor variables and age as the criterion in each case. These analyses were designed to determine linear relationships between age and each group of predictor variables: We wished to determine whether the predictors could distinguish the older from the younger adolescents. Age was treated as a continuous variable because discrete changes were not expected from year to year. By treating age as the criterion variable in the analyses, we were able to enter both continuous and categorical variables as predictors. This data analytic approach also allowed an investigation of the unique variance each of the predictors shared with age, while controlling for overlap among them, and it resulted in fewer analyses being done, thereby reducing the risk of Type I error.

RESULTS

Characteristics of Homeless Youth. A majority of the adolescents were female and about half were 14 or 15 years old (see Table 1). The sample was racially mixed and included large numbers of white and African-American adolescents (due to their small numbers, youth of other ethnic backgrounds were considered in analyses along with the African-Americans). Many of the youth had repeated a grade (n = 39; 32.0%) and some had quit school (n = 14; 11.5%). Most of the adolescents came from working-class families, with many parents employed as laborers or in other unskilled or blue-collar occupations. Much smaller percentages had parents with professional or managerial backgrounds. Most of the homeless adolescents had parents who had graduated from high school and a fair number of the parents had some college experience. Most of the adolescents had been homeless only once and, in their current episode, were homeless for one week or less. Furthermore, most of the sample reported having been homeless for three weeks or less total in their lives. Some had spent time living on the streets (n = 11; 9.0%). Almost half of the adolescents had run away from home, with smaller numbers reporting having been forced to leave by their parents ("throwaways") or were at the shelter with their parents' understanding that they would seek some services and then return home ("intervention seekers"). No seasonal differences were found on any key measures.

DSM-III-R diagnoses derived from the DISC indicated high rates for all major categories (see Table 2), including disruptive behavior disorders, depression and dysthymia, mania and hypomania, drug abuse/dependence, and alcohol abuse/dependence. Psychosis was rare in this sample, as in most other adolescent samples. Considering diagnostic subtypes, it was found that most of the disruptive behavior disorders were accounted for by conduct disorder and most of the drug abuse/dependence involved marijuana. Both within and across major diagnostic categories, there was overlap among certain disorders. Thus, for example, most of the youth with depression also showed dysthymia (70.0%) and many youth showing drug abuse/dependence also showed alcohol abuse/dependence (44.8%).

Age Differences. Prior to conducting the main analyses, bivariate correlations were computed to determine whether there was a significant relationship between age and three basic demographic variables: gender, race, and parent's occupation-based socioeconomic status (Stevens & Featherman, 1981). The point-biserial correlation between gender and age was significant (r = .21, p < .05), with homeless female adolescents tending to be younger than males (p > .25 for the correlations involving race

TABLE 1. Background characteristics of homeless youth (N = 122)

Age	n	Percent
12	5	4.1
13	22	18.0
14	25	20.5
15	39	32.0
16	18	14.5
17	13	10.7
Gender		
Male	39	32.0
Female	83	68.0
Race		
White	55	45.1
African-American	56	45.9
Other	11	9.0
Parental occupation-based SES[a]		
Unskilled	54	47.8
Blue collar	25	22.1
Managerial	20	17.7
Professional	14	12.4
Parental education[a]		
Less than high school	21	17.8
High school graduate	44	37.3
Some college	35	29.7
College degree	18	15.3
Adolescent's educational level		
6th or below	12	9.9
7th	23	18.9
8th	29	23.8
9th	27	22.1
10th	19	15.6
11th	6	4.9
12th	6	4.9

Boesky, Toro, and Bukowski

Reason homeless (current episode)	n	Percent
Runaway	56	46.7
Throwaway	32	26.7
Intervention seeker	32	26.7
Time homeless (current episode)		
1-7 days	82	67.2
8-14 days	24	19.7
15 days-2 months	10	8.2
3-36 months	6	4.8
Homeless episodes (lifetime)	n	Percent
1	81	66.4
2	13	10.7
3-4	18	14.7
5 or more	10	8.1

[a]Due to missing data, the sample available on these variables is less than the full $\underline{N}$ = 122.

and socioeconomic status). Because of this significant effect, gender was entered first in all further analyses.

The first of the nine hierarchical multiple regression analyses included the four CTS scales as predictors and indicated that older adolescents used more verbal aggression against their parents. A second analysis using the four FES scales as predictors revealed that younger homeless adolescents reported more cohesive families. A third analysis involving the three ICE factors found no age effects. However, an analysis using the three ICE variables assessing abuse and neglect indicated that older homeless adolescents had experienced more sexual abuse. An analysis involving items from the HES revealed that the older homeless adolescents were more likely to be throwaways than the younger adolescents. In addition, the older adolescents had spent more time homeless in their lifetimes. The regression analyses for the three SNI indices and the three self-efficacy/self-esteem variables revealed no age differences. When diagnostic categories from the DISC were entered into another analysis, results indicated that more of the older homeless adolescents met criteria for Drug Abuse/Dependence. When the BSI global severity index and total scores on the PHC and MLEI were entered into a final analysis, it was found that the

TABLE 2. DSM-III-R diagnoses for homeless youth (N = 122)

	n	Percent	n	Percent
Depression/Dysthymia	40	32.8		
Depression			30	24.6
Dysthymia			31	25.4
Mania/Hypomania	29	23.8		
Mania			15	12.3
Hypomania			14	11.5
Psychosis	1	0.8		
Disruptive Behavior	59	48.4		
Attention Deficit			9	7.4
Oppositional Defiant			9	7.4
Conduct Disorder			49	40.2
Alcohol Abuse/Dependence	26	21.3		
Abuse			3	2.5
Dependence			23	18.9
Drug Abuse/Dependence	29	23.8		
Marijuana Abuse			5	4.1
Marijuana Dependence			21	17.2
Amphetamines			5	4.1
Barbituates/Tranquilizers			1	0.8
Opiates			3	2.5
Cocaine			3	2.5
Hallucinogens			4	3.3
Inhalants			3	2.5
Other			3	2.5

older homeless adolescents had experienced a greater number of recent stressful life events (see Table 3).

DISCUSSION

The present study provided data on a representative sample of homeless adolescents and investigated age differences among them. Demographic

TABLE 3. Significant results from nine regression analyses: Age as criterion

Predictors	Simple r	β	sr^2	F
Family environment				
Cohesion	−.19	−.23	.05	6.76*
Family violence				
Sexual abuse	.13	.23	.05	5.86*
Child verbal aggression	.19	.25	.06	7.82**
Psychiatric diagnoses				
Drug abuse/dependence	.31	.30	.09	12.17**
Stressful life events				
Total events	.31	.29	.08	11.33**
History of homelessness				
Throwaway[a]	.25	.20	.04	5.49*
Total time homeless	.21	.19	.03	4.55*

Note. Because of its relationship with age, gender was treated as a covariate in all analyses. The simple rs are Pearson correlation coefficients. The sr^2 s are squared semi-partial correlation coefficients indicating the percent of unique criterion age variance accounted for by each predictor variable (controlling for gender and other predictors already entered). The βs are the associated standarized regression coefficients and indicate the direction of the relationship between age and each predictor. The Fs test whether βs (and sr^2 s) differ from zero.
[a] This contrast is one of two entered to assess the relationship of reason for homelessness to age and indicates that throwaways were older than the other two groups (0.6 years older than runaways and 0.9 years older than intervention seekers).

*p < .05   **p < .01

characteristics of the sample were similar to previous studies of homeless adolescents (e.g., Robertson, 1990). Most homeless adolescents in our sample came from poor to working class backgrounds, with small numbers coming from middle to upper-class and professional backgrounds. Previous studies vary on the racial distribution of their samples, depending on the areas in which the studies were conducted. The racial distribution observed in the present study reflects an overrepresentation of minority individuals compared to the population of the metropolitan area where the study was conducted (54.9% nonwhite compared to 20.1% in the general population). Nonwhites, especially African-Americans, appear to be over-represented in the adolescent homeless population, as they are in the adult homeless population (North & Smith, 1994; Rossi, 1990).

In addition to the commonly-cited subgroups of runaways and throw-aways, this study identified a third group of "intervention seekers," youth who are temporarily seeking help. This group may be a more recent phenomenon associated with the growing visibility of youth shelters in most metropolitan areas. Other data from this study indicated that most homeless youth have been homeless for a very short period of time. In fact, two thirds of the sample had been homeless for a week or less in their current episode of homelessness. However, many (33.6%) had also been homeless before.

Several studies have been conducted in large cities where samples consisted of homeless adolescents staying at an "improvised shelter" or "on the streets." These samples tend to have a somewhat different profile from samples of homeless adolescents utilizing shelters. Many of the samples in such studies have also included an older group of homeless adolescents, ranging up to 21 years of age, as well as a majority of males (Cauce et al., 1994; Robertson, 1990). These street samples also appear to include adolescents and young adults who have been homeless longer than those in the present study. Homeless adolescents receiving services from youth shelters appear to be younger, include more girls, and are homeless for shorter periods of time. The studies of "street youth," like those of homeless young adults, also sometimes find greater degrees of pathology (e.g., substance abuse, criminal behavior) than observed in our shelter sample. Future research on homeless adolescents needs to pay careful attention to the characteristics of the samples obtained and qualify the generalizability of its results. In the case of the present study, the findings may not apply to youth spending most of their time on the streets nor to those who are 18 or older.

Though no normative data are yet available based on the Diagnostic Interview Schedule for Children (DISC), rates for all DSM-III-R disorders assessed appeared high. The high rates for disruptive behavior disorders were not surprising, given that adolescent homelessness and delinquency have long been considered as closely connected phenomenon. However, the rates for depression and mania were also high, suggesting the need to attend to the mental health needs of homeless youth in addition to their delinquent tendencies. The rates for drug and alcohol abuse/dependence, though high, may not have been as high as some might have expected in a homeless youth sample and the use of drugs other than marijuana was relatively rare. This difference between public perception and the data obtained in this study may be the result of the overemphasis in both research and the media on street youth, a small but very visible subgroup who may have more substance abuse problems.

A set of key analyses assessed relationships between the age of homeless adolescents (ranging from 12 to 17 years) and various other characteristics. Age was related to gender, with females tending to be younger than males. Since other studies have not investigated this topic, it's difficult to assess whether such a relationship exists among homeless adolescents in other locations. However, if the relationship does hold elsewhere, these data are interesting when combined with our understanding of the characteristics of homeless young adults. A variety of studies in many locations find that males clearly predominate among homeless adults (e.g., Rossi, 1990; Toro et al., 1995; Toro & Wall, 1991). Thus, with increasing age, the risk of homelessness for males may increase, while decreasing for females.

On several indices, a positive relationship between age and psychosocial variables was found, such that the older homeless adolescents were more disturbed. It may be that older homeless adolescents have had more time to expose themselves to certain situations than younger adolescents, by virtue of their age. Thus, finding that older homeless adolescents report relatively more sexual abuse could partly be due to having had more opportunity to experience this type of abuse as they age and become more sexually active. Similarly, the older homeless adolescents also reported a higher rate of drug abuse/dependence. This may have been due to an increased opportunity for exposure to various illicit substances. This outcome is consistent with recent studies suggesting that drug use in the general population increases as adolescents become older (Elliot, Huizinga, & Menard, 1989; Rice, 1984).

Adolescents forced to leave home tended to be older than those who ran away or were simply seeking services. As adolescents get older, they become less physically and psychologically dependent on their parents. Perhaps it is easier for parents to force out older adolescents, who may also be more seriously engaged in a struggle for autonomy than their younger counterparts. Younger adolescents also reported more cohesive families than older adolescents. This is consistent with the idea that the younger adolescents are more dependent and closer to their parents. The observed association between age and reason for homelessness has other implications for intervention as well as for future research. Prior studies that have investigated runaway/throwaway subgroups have rarely investigated age effects and the one study that did also found throwaways to be older than runaways (Adams, Gullotta & Clancy, 1985). However, investigators did not control for these age effects in subsequent analyses. This lack of attention to the relationship between age and subgroup leads one to question whether differences between runaway and throwaway adolescents would continue to be evident after controlling for age. Those designing interventions need to be aware that throwaway youth will not only have special needs because of their particular family dynamics, but also because of their age. For example, such youth may not be able to return home but may be old enough that independent living is a viable option.

Though significant relationships were found between age and eight predictors (including gender), the size of these relationships was generally modest (accounting for only 3-9% of age variance) and relationships were not found between age and other psychosocial variables. This outcome may be due to the adolescent's current condition of homelessness. Homeless adolescents may differ with regard to some of these psychosocial variables when compared to their non-homeless counterparts, but differences within the homeless population may not be as large. For example, studies comparing homeless adolescents to matched samples of non-homeless adolescents have found the homeless adolescents to report more physical abuse, parental rejection and hostile control (Wolfe, 1994). However, none of these studies investigated differences among homeless adolescents of various ages. Self-esteem may be low for all homeless adolescents, regardless of their age. Wolk and Brandon (1977) found that homeless youth were more self-doubting than their non-homeless counterparts and others have found homeless adolescents to have lower self-esteem, poorer self-images, and higher rates of depression and other psychopathology than non-homeless youth (Maxwell, 1992; Wolfe, 1994). Being homeless may override some of the developmental differences in psychosocial variables seen in the general adolescent population. The lack of age differences on many variables in the present study may also have been due to the recent blurring of early and late adolescence as well as young adulthood. Perhaps the age range of 12 to 17 was not large enough to detect all of the developmental differences associated with this period of life. Though investigators find few homeless youth under age 12, there are many in late adolescence and early adulthood.

Results from the present study could have several implications for research and intervention with homeless adolescents. At least among those staying in shelters, the over-representation of girls, 14-15 year-old youth, and minority groups need to be considered. For example, interventions attempting to prevent teen homelessness would do well to target youth 14 or younger as well as poor urban areas with high concentrations of African-Americans and other minority groups. Shafer and Caton (1991) considered the effect age has on interventions with homeless youth and proposed that younger homeless adolescents may benefit most from family-oriented services. It has been reported that family treatment is a common and effective method of intervention among homeless adolescents (Jones, 1988; Ostensen, 1981). Our results suggest that family therapy may be beneficial for both older and younger homeless youth and not necessarily more appropriate for specific issues associated with early adolescence. One of the most common features that emerges when homeless adolescents have been compared to non-homeless youth, is the extent of conflict, violence, and disorganization seen in the families of the homeless (Wolfe, 1994). Such features further indicate the value of a family-oriented approach for homeless adolescents of all ages.

Although the reliability of self-report of mental health problems and drug use among adolescents has been documented (Costello & Angold, 1988; O'Malley, Bachman & Johnston, 1983), an exclusive reliance on this type of assessment is a limitation of our study. Direct observational measures could contribute additional information. Although participants in our sample were collected from all the major shelters in the area, this reliance on a shelter population and the lack of homeless adolescents living on the streets limits generalizability. Finally, the study's cross-sectional design did not allow an investigation of age differences independent of cohort effects.

Future investigators should continue to utilize reliable and valid measures and to include both shelter and street samples. Future studies assessing age differences among homeless youth may want to include individuals in their late teens and early twenties. Homeless adolescents have been shown to be at higher risk for difficulties later in life, including homelessness as adults (Windle, 1989). To date, only a few longitudinal studies of homeless youth have been done (Olson et al., 1980; Windle, 1989). More such research is sorely needed if we are to understand the long-term outcomes for this important group of at-risk youth. In addition to the need for more research generally, there is a need for carefully evaluated interventions. Though treatment programs for homeless adolescents have been developing at a rapid pace in the past two decades, we have virtually no high quality evaluations of such programs (with one notable exception, Cauce et al., 1994). Prevention programs targeted toward homelessness are virtually nonexistent. More intervention research of all types is desperately needed if we are to reduce the incidence of adolescent homelessness in our society.

REFERENCES

Adams, G. R., Gullotta, T., & Clancy, M. A. (1985). Homeless adolescents: A descriptive study of similarities and differences between runaways and throwaways. *Adolescence, 20,* 715-724.
Cauce, A. M., Morgan, C. J., Wagner, V., Moore, E., Sy, J., Wurzbacher, K.,

Weeden, K., Tomlin, S., & Blanchard, T. (1994). Effectiveness of intensive case management for homeless adolescents: Results of a 3-month follow-up. *Journal of Emotional and Behavioral Disorders, 2*(4), 219-227.

Corcoran, K., & Fisher, J. (1987). *Measures for clinical practice: A sourcebook.* New York: The Free Press.

Costello, E. J., & Angold, A. (1988). Scales to assess child and adolescent depression: Checklists, screens, and nets. *Journal of the American Academy of Child and Adolescent Psychiatry, 27*, 726-737.

Costello, E. J., Edelbrock, C., & Costello, A. J. (1985). Validity of the NIMH Diagnostic Interview Schedule for Children: A comparison between psychiatric and pediatric referrals. *Journal of Abnormal Child Psychology, 13*, 579-595.

Derogatis, L. R. & Melisaratos, N. (1983). The Brief Symptom Inventory: An introductory report. *Psychological Medicine, 13*, 595-605.

Elliot, D. S., Huizinga, D., & Menard, S. (1989). *Multiple problem youth: Delinquency, substance use, and mental health problems.* New York: Springer-Verlag.

Hombs, M. E. (1990). *American homelessness: A reference handbook.* Santa Barbara: ABC-CLIO.

Jones, L. P. (1988). A typology of adolescent runaways. *Child and Adolescent Social Work, 5*(1), 16-29.

Lovell, A. M. (1984). *Modified Life Events Interview.* Unpublished Manuscript, Epidemiology of Mental Disorders Research Department, New York State Psychiatric Institute, New York, NY.

Maxwell, B. E. (1992). Hostility, depression, and self-esteem among troubled and homeless adolescents in crisis. *Journal of Youth and Adolescence, 2*, 139-150.

Moos, R. H., & Moos, B. S. (1986). *Family Environment Scale manual (second edition).* Palo Alto, CA: Consulting Psychologists Press.

Morse, G., & Calsyn, R. J. (1986). Mentally ill homeless people in St. Louis: Needy, willing but underserved. *International Journal of Mental Health, 14*, 74-94.

North, C. S., & Smith, E. M. (1994). Comparison of white and nonwhite homeless men and women. *Social Work, 39*, 639-647.

Olson, L., Liebow, E., Mannino, F. & Shore, M. (1980). Runaway children twelve years later: A follow up. *Journal of Family Issues, 1*, 165-188.

O'Malley, P. M., Bachman, J. G., & Johnston, L. D. (1983). Reliability and consistency in self-reports of drug use. *International Journal of the Addictions, 18*, 805-824.

Ostensen, K. W. (1981). The runaway crisis: Is family therapy the answer? *American Journal of Family Therapy, 9*, 3-12.

Rabideau, J. M. P., & Toro, P.A. (in press, 1996). Social and environmental predictors of adjustment in homeless children. *Journal of Prevention & Intervention in the Community.*

Rice, F. P. (1984). *The Adolescent: Development, relationships, and culture.* Boston: Allyn & Bacon.

Ringwalt, C. L., Greene, J. M., & Iachan, R. (November, 1994). Prevalence and characteristics of youth in households with runaway and homeless experience. Meeting of the American Public Health Association, Washington, DC.

Robertson, M. J. (1990, August). Characteristics and circumstances of homeless adolescents in Hollywood. Paper presented at the annual meeting of the American Psychological Association, Boston, MA.

Robertson, M. J. (1991). Homeless youth: An overview of the recent literature. In J. H. Dryder-Coe, L. M. Salamon, & J. M. Molnar (Eds.), *Homeless children and youth: A new American dilemma* (pp. 33-68). Baltimore: Johns Hopkins Press.

Rosenberg, M. (1965). *Society and the adolescent self-image.* Princeton: Princeton University Press.

Rossi, P. H. (1990). The old homeless and the new homeless in historical perspective. *American Psychologist, 45,* 954-959.

Shaffer, D. & Caton, C. L. M. (1984). *Runaway and homeless youth in New York City: A report to the Ittleson Foundation.* New York: New York State Psychiatric Institute and Columbia University.

Shaffer, D., Schwab-Stone, M., Fisher, P. C., Piacentini, J., Davies, M., Conners, C.K., & Regier, D. (1993). The Diagnostic Interview Schedule for Children-Revised version (DISC-R): Preparation, field testing, interrater reliability, and acceptability. *Journal of the American Academy of Child and Adolescent Psychiatry, 32,* 643-650.

Sherer, M., Maddux, J. E., Mercandante, B., Prentice-Dunn, S., Jacobs, B., & Rogers, R. W. (1982). The Self-Efficacy Scale: Construction and validation. *Psychological Reports, 31,* 663-671.

Stevens, G., & Featherman, D. L. (1981). A revised socioeconomic index of occupational status. *Social Science Research, 10,* 364-395.

Straus, M. (1990). The Conflict Tactics Scales and its critics: An evaluation and new data on validity and reliability. In M. A. Straus & R. J. Gelles, *Physical violence in American families: Risk factors and adaptations to violence in 8,145 families.* New Brunswick, NJ: Transaction Press.

Straus, M. A., Gelles, R. J., & Steinmetz, S. K. (1980). *Behind closed doors: Violence in the American family.* New York: Doubleday/Anchor.

Toro, P. A., Bellavia, C., Daeschler, C., Owens, B., Wall, D. D., Passero, J. M., & Thomas, D. M. (1995). Distinguishing homelessness from poverty: A comparative study. *Journal of Consulting and Clinical Psychology, 63,* 280-289.

Toro, P. A., & McDonell, D. M. (1992). Beliefs, attitudes, and knowledge about homelessness: A survey of the general public. *American Journal of Community Psychology, 20,* 53-80.

Toro, P. A., & Wall, D. D. (1991). Research on homeless persons: Diagnostic comparisons and practice implications. *Professional Psychology: Research and Practice, 22,* 479-488.

Windle, M. (1989). Substance use and abuse among adolescent runaways: A four-year follow-up study. *Journal of Youth and Adolescence, 18,* 331-344.

Wolfe, S. M. (August, 1994). A comparative study of housed and homeless adolescents. 102nd Annual Convention, American Psychological Association, Los Angeles.

Wolfe, S. M., & Toro, P. A. (1992). *People and transitions in housing (PATH) project: Pilot reliability study.* Unpublished report, Department of Psychology, Wayne State University, Detroit, MI.

Wolk, S. & Brandon, J. (1977). Runaway adolescents' perceptions of parents and self. *Adolescence, 12,* 175-188.

Zozus, R.T., & Zax, M. (1991). Perceptions of childhood: Exploring possible etiological factors in homelessness. *Hospital and Community Psychiatry, 42,* 535-537.

Characteristics of Homeless Women with Dependent Children: A Controlled Study

Patricia D. LaVesser
Elizabeth M. Smith
Susan Bradford

Washington University School of Medicine

INTRODUCTION

The fastest growing group in the homeless population is families with dependent children (Hausman & Hammen, 1993; Nunez, 1994; Waxman, 1994), which account for 39% of the homeless population (Waxman, 1994). The same study found that children comprise over one-fourth of the homeless. A separate study related to service demand for homeless people conducted between 1990 and 1992 reported that the largest increase in demand was from families with children (National Coalition for the Homeless, 1992). The majority of homeless families are headed by single women (Nunez, 1994).

Poverty and a lack of affordable housing are consistently related to

Address correspondence to: Elizabeth M. Smith, Washington University School of Medicine, Department of Psychiatry, 4940 Children's Place, St. Louis, MO 63110.

This research was supported by National Institute on Alcohol Abuse and Alcoholism Grant AA08335.

[Haworth co-indexing entry note]: "Characteristics of Homeless Women with Dependent Children: A Controlled Study." LaVesser, Patricia D., Elizabeth M. Smith, and Susan Bradford. Co-published simultaneously in *Journal of Prevention & Intervention in the Community* (The Haworth Press, Inc.) Vol. 15, No. 2, 1997, pp. 37-52; and: *Diversity Within the Homeless Population: Implications for Intervention* (ed: Elizabeth M. Smith, and Joseph R. Ferrari) The Haworth Press, Inc., 1997, pp. 37-52. Single or multiple copies of this article are available for a fee from The Haworth Document Delivery Service [1-800-342-9678, 9:00 a.m. - 5:00 p.m. (EST). E-mail address: getinfo@haworth.com].

family homelessness (Koegel, Melamid, & Burnam, 1995). However, factors that differentiate homeless families from the very poor who remain housed are less clearly defined (Johnson, 1988). How does a mother "at risk" for being homeless differ from mothers with children who are actually homeless? Only a few studies have systematically compared homeless and housed families in an attempt to identify some of the unique correlates of family homelessness.

Bassuk and Rosenberg (1988) found that a history of family violence and fragmented social support were two factors that distinguished 49 homeless mothers in Boston from 81 long-term female welfare recipients in public housing. Wood, Valdez, Hayashi and Shen (1990) reported similar findings on a larger sample of 196 homeless and 194 housed families in Los Angeles. They also identified drug use and mental health problems as significantly more common among the homeless families. In their study, only half of the homeless families were headed by single mothers. Single-parent homeless families reported many more relationship problems, such as drug abuse or violence, than did two-parent homeless families. The housed poor sample was obtained from families presenting to four welfare offices and was selected on the basis of relative housing stability.

In contrast, Goodman (1991a) found no differences in physical or sexual abuse between 50 homeless and 50 housed poor mothers in New England. She also found no differences between these same homeless and housed respondents on any social support variables with the exception of the degree to which they expressed trust in their social networks (Goodman, 1991b). The findings of Shinn, Knickman and Weitzman (1991) parallel Goodman's in that they describe only minimal differences in the number of reported social ties between a group of 677 homeless mothers and 495 housed mothers in New York City. However, they did find differences between the housed and homeless families in reports of childhood sexual abuse, adult physical abuse, and past mental hospitalization (Weitzman, Knickman, & Shinn, 1992). In both studies, housed families were selected randomly from the total pool of families receiving Aid for Families with Dependent Children (AFDC) in their respective cities. Goodman (1991a; 1991b) recruited homeless families from meetings they were required to attend at the local welfare office, while Shinn and colleagues (1991) identified homeless families at the time they requested shelter at one of New York City's Emergency Assistance Points.

Several studies that used general population information for comparison to the homeless population have further identified victimization, mental illness, and substance abuse as more prevalent or "overrepresented" in homeless families (Breakey et al. 1989; Browne, 1993; D'Ercole &

Struening, 1990; Goodman, Dutton, & Harris, 1995; Robertson, 1991; Zima, Wells, Benjamin, & Duan, in press). Other research has identified childhood experiences such as out-of-home placement, tenure in public housing, and homelessness as risk factors for adult homelessness (Koegel, Melamid, & Burnam, 1995), again using general population information for comparison. These studies suggest that there are specific characteristics that can aid in determining who among the poor become homeless.

In this paper, we first identify specific demographic, childhood and family, marital, and mental health or substance abuse factors that distinguish a group of homeless women from a randomly-selected sample of low-income housed women in St. Louis. Results of this study are compared to the results of other studies, and their implications for policy related to intervention and potential prevention of family homelessness are discussed.

METHODS

Sampling. The study sample was drawn from 300 homeless women who participated in a previous epidemiologic study of the homeless in St. Louis between October 1989 and September 1990 (Smith, North, & Spitznagel, 1992). Participants were considered homeless if they had no stable residence and were currently staying in a public shelter or in an unsheltered location without a personal mailing address, such as on the streets, in a car, in an abandoned building, or in a bus station. The sample was drawn from all overnight and daytime shelters in St. Louis that did not specialize in serving particular subgroups of women, such as pregnant women or abused women. Eighty-two percent of night shelters, and 100% of the day shelters cooperated in the study. Because each shelter tended to attract a slightly different subpopulation of the homeless, sampling was conducted proportionally to the number of persons in the various programs. The list of shelters was randomized, and a set of random numbers was generated by computer to select subjects from the daily log of residents occupying beds in the night shelters or attending the day shelters. Interviewing was conducted at the various sites at different times during the month. Since all study participants were randomly sampled during all four seasons, it is believed that the sample was representative of all homeless women in St. Louis shelters.

The majority of the homeless women who participated in the previous study (247 of 300) had children under 17 years of age. Interviews were completed with 202 women; 16 had moved out of the area; 20 could not be located; two were deceased; and one was in a psychiatric hospital and unable to give informed consent for an interview. Only six women refused to participate. The overall rate was 82%.

The control sample was selected from the neighborhoods where the homeless mothers had lived just prior to their most recent episode of homelessness and enlistment in the epidemiologic study. Households in these neighborhoods were surveyed to identify prospective subjects for the comparison group. The women were matched in age (within five years) to a case mother from that same neighborhood and were screened to ascertain that they had never been homeless and that they had one or more natural-born children under age 17 living with them. One hundred and fourteen housed women who met these criteria and were willing to participate were included in the study.

Measures. A modified version of the Diagnostic Interview Schedule (DIS) (Robins, Helzer, Croughan, Williams, & Spitzer, 1981) used in the previous study of the case mothers was administered to the control mothers during the current study. The DIS permitted the establishment of certain DSM-III-R (American Psychiatric Association, 1987) diagnoses in these women, including depression, bipolar affective disorder, alcohol abuse/dependence, drug abuse/dependence, panic disorder, generalized anxiety disorder, posttraumatic stress disorder, schizophrenia, and antisocial personality disorder. Sections on these disorders were included in the interview because they were considered to be relatively common disorders (Robins & Regier, 1991).

A structured interview designed for the project was administered to all of the case mothers and the control mothers. Information was obtained on: pregnancy histories, including maternal use of tobacco, alcohol, drugs and medical care; each living child's developmental history, early relationships with caregivers, patterns of physical or sexual abuse, and medical history; and family functioning and social support network availability.

Cognitive functioning of each of the mothers was assessed using the Kaufman Brief Intelligence Test (K-BIT) (Kaufman & Kaufman, 1990). This 130-item scale is divided into two subtests: Vocabulary (45 Expressive Vocabulary items and 37 Definitions) and Matrices (48 items). It was nationally standardized on a large, well-stratified sample.

Data Analysis. To identify significant differences between the two groups of women at the bivariate level, the Pearson chi-square test and t-test were used. Demographic variables (e.g., marital status, education and family size), family history and childhood experiences (i.e., being placed in foster care or institutionalized as a minor, leaving home before age 17 and being a victim of child abuse), lifetime DIS/DSM-III-R psychiatric diagnostic rates, and cognitive ability as measured by the K-BIT were the variables examined for differences. Associations between the variables under study were identified using Spearman correlation for dichotomous variables and Pearson r for the age and count variables.

To investigate the link between crack/cocaine use and women and children becoming homeless, drug data received extra consideration. Drug users were separated into two mutually exclusive groups: those who had ever used crack/cocaine and those who had only used other drugs. Likewise, drug abuse or dependence was not coded in one dichotomous variable but divided between cocaine abuse/dependence and other positive drug diagnoses. Therefore, four dichotomous drug variables were used: (1) any cocaine use; (2) any drug use other than cocaine; (3) any cocaine abuse/dependence; and (4) any drug abuse/dependence other than cocaine abuse/dependence. Variables distinguishing the homeless from the housed women at the bivariate level were entered into stepwise logistic regression to develop a multivariate model of homelessness (Fleiss, Williams, & Dubro, 1986). SAS statistical software (SAS Institute, 1996) was used for all computations.

RESULTS

Demographics. The demographic characteristics of the mothers are shown in Table I. The majority of women in both samples were African-American and the mean age was 29.4 ± 6.1 (median age = 29). Although the mothers were similar in terms of age, case mothers had more children than control mothers, t (287.4) = 4.5, $p < .001$. They were less likely to be married [χ^2 (1, $n = 316$) = 19.6, $p = .001$], to have completed high school [χ^2 (1, $n = 316$) = 5.2, $p = .02$], and to be employed [χ^2 (1, $n = 316$) = 4.8, $p = .03$]. Since more homeless than housed women obtained their 12th grade education with a high school equivalency (GED), there was a more dramatic difference in the school dropout rates, χ^2 (1, $n = 316$) = 14.2, $p = .001$.

The K-BIT was completed by 195 (96.5%) of the case mothers in the study and 112 (98%) of the control mothers. The standardized composite score was skewed for both samples with few control mothers and none of the case mothers scoring above the average range. Significantly more case mothers scored below average, χ^2 (1, $n = 307$) = 7.6, $p = .006$ (Table I).

Household Composition. As seen in Table II, the women were living in many different types of households at the time of the interview. Almost half (47%) of the women headed single-parent households, and 55% of these single-parent households were in Section 8 housing. Case mothers were more likely to be single head of households [χ^2 (1, $n = 316$) = 11.4,

TABLE I. Demographics

	CASE N = 202		CONTROL N = 114	
	N	%	N	%
RACE				
African American	182	90.10	98	85.96
MARITAL STATUS				
Married	13	6.44	27	23.68***
Widowed	2	0.99	2	1.75
Separated	46	22.77	18	15.79
Divorced	15	7.43	12	10.53
Never Married	126	62.38*	55	48.25
EDUCATION				
Any college	7	3.47	12	10.53
H.S. diploma	69	34.16	53	46.49
G.E.D.	32	15.84	11	9.65
No H.S. equivalency	94	46.53*	38	33.33
Dropped out of school	119	58.91***	42	36.84
KBIT composite score is average or above	63	32.31	54	48. 21**
EMPLOYMENT HISTORY				
Currently working	34	16.83	31	27. 19*
Never worked fulltime	24	13.19	24	21.05
Longest job < 1 year	112	61.54	75	65.79
	RANGE	MEAN ± STD	RANGE	MEAN ± STD
Current Age	19-56	29.3 ± 6.2	18-51	29.5 ± 6.0
Age First Homeless	9-48	25.4 ± 6.5	–	–
Age at First Livebirth	13-36	18.2 ± 3.4	12-32	19.2 ± 4.3
Age at First Pregnancy*	13-36	17.7 ± 3.2	12-32	18.6 ± 3.9
Number of Children***	1-9	3.2 ± 1.6	1-6	2.5 ± 1.2
Years of Education**	8-16	11.2 ± 1.4	7-17	11.7 ± 1.7

* $p < .05$
** $p \leq .01$
*** $p \leq .001$

$p = .001$]. Case mothers were no more likely than control mothers to be living in "doubled-up" situations but were less likely to be renting market-rate housing or to be buying the property where they lived. Twenty-one case mothers (10.4%) were still homeless, (i.e., in shelters, institutions, transitional housing or moving from place to place), and fourteen of

TABLE II. Household Composition

	CASE N = 202		CONTROL N = 114	
	N	%	N	%
TYPE OF HOUSING				
Homeless	8	3.96	—	—
Institution	3	1.49	—	—
Mover	3	1.49	—	—
Transition	7	3.47	—	—
Doubled-up	30	14.85	15	13.16
Rental	57	28.22	52	45.61
Section 8	89	44.06	21	18.42
Mortgage	5	2.48	26	22.81
RESPONDENT LIVES WITH				
Alone	19	9.41	—	—
Children only	109	53.96***	39	34.21
Relatives	35	17.33	29	25.44
Spouse	5	2.48	24	21.05
Partner	22	10.89	12	10.53
In-laws[1]	1	0.50	2	1.75
Friend	6	2.97	1	0.88
Hosts relative, friend or in-law	5	2.48	7	6.14
—With her children	168	83.17	114	100.00*
—With her husband	6	2.97	26	22.81*
—With a partner	26	12.87	18	15.79
	RANGE	MEAN ± STD	RANGE	MEAN ± STD
Total Household Members	1-12	4.1 ± 2.2	2-9	4.5 ± 1.6
Adult[2] Household Members*	1-5	1.5 ± 0.8	1-5	1.9 ± 0.9
Children Under 18 years of age	0-9	2.5 ± 1.9	1-6	2.6 ± 1.2

*p < .05
***p < .001

[1]"In-laws" includes partners' relatives.
[2]18 years of age and older

these women had their children with them. Seventeen percent of the case mothers were not living with their children.

Pregnancy and Childbirth Histories. The pregnancy and childbearing histories of the two groups of women were similar. The case mothers' first pregnancy occurred between the ages of 13 and 36, and 85% resulted in livebirth, 5% elective abortion, 8% miscarriage, and 2% stillbirth or ectopic pregnancy. The control mothers' first pregnancy occurred between the ages of 12 and 32, and 85% resulted in livebirth, 4% elective abortion, 7% miscarriage, and 4% stillbirth or ectopic pregnancy. Case mothers were first pregnant at earlier ages than the control mothers, t (197) = 2.1, p = .03 (Table I).

The case mothers also delivered their first livebirth one year younger than controls but this difference is not significant, t (201.2) = 1.9, p = .06 (Table I). The proportion who gave birth before their 18th birthday was nearly identical in both samples (49% vs. 48%). These teenage mothers were younger than the rest of the sample (t (313) = 2.6, p = .01), 59% of them never married, and 10% were married at time of interview. The teenage mothers who never married were younger than those who had, t (152) = 5.1, p < .001). One-fourth (24.4%) of the case mothers were childless on their 20th birthday compared to 36.8% of the control mothers, χ^2 (1, n = 315) = 5.5, p = .02.

Partners/Biological Fathers. There was little difference between the samples in the reports of spousal abuse. Thirty-one percent of the homeless women and 28% of the housed women said a partner had inflicted physical injury; adding threats of violence increased these proportions to 40% vs. 32.5%. Case mothers reported one to seven sexual partners were biological fathers of their children (mean = 2.0 ± 1.1) compared to one to four fathers reported by the control mothers (mean = 1.6 ± 0.8), t (298.5) = 3.86, p < .001.

Social Support Network. Fourteen case mothers and two control mothers said they had no supports, and one control mother refused to answer questions regarding her social support network. Most of the women in both groups (76.7% cases and 79.6% controls) reported at least one dependable support, someone who gave help with food, money, shelter, childcare, or other everyday needs. There were no differences in the total number of supports (3.3 ± 1.9 vs. 3.6 ± 1.7) or the number of dependable supports (1.9 ± 1.6 vs. 2.0 ± 1.6) reported by the women.

Mothers' Childhood. Family environment variables from the mothers' childhood are shown in Table III. Most of the women had a father figure. Over three-fourths of the childhood homes received support from a male wage earner (father, step-father or mother's boyfriend), however, more case mothers' families received welfare income χ^2 (1, n = 313) = 4.4, p = .04. A larger proportion of homeless women had spent time in a foster home, group home, or juvenile detention center χ^2 (1, n = 316) = 5.9, p = .02. Homeless women were also more likely to have left home before age 17, χ^2 (1, n = 316) = 6.8, p = .01.

Somewhat higher proportions of the case mothers reported being on the receiving end of physical violence. Reports of physical abuse included being kicked or hit with a fist or object, burns, and being threatened with a weapon. Reports of emotional abuse included threats of abandonment, verbal abuse, throwing or hitting an object, the silent treatment, and being locked in a closet. The women were asked if they were ever sexually abused as a child or teenager, and "Before the age of 18, did any adult . . . touch you or make you touch them in a sexual way when you did not want to . . . ?" The homeless women reported more childhood sexual molestation [χ^2 (1, n = 316) = 5.6, p = .02] and more emotional abuse [χ^2 (1, n = 316) = 4.6, p = .03], but reported rates of physical abuse did not differ. An extremely high proportion of the homeless women reported at least one of the three kinds of child abuse χ^2 (1, n = 316) = 9.5, p = .002.

Psychiatric Disorders. Rates of lifetime psychiatric disorders are shown in Table IV.

Axis I Disorders. Case mothers were more likely than controls to have a lifetime diagnosis of depression [χ^2 (1, n = 316) = 7.3, p < .01] and more likely to have a lifetime diagnosis of Posttraumatic Stress Disorder (PTSD) [χ^2 (1, n = 312) = 16.4, p = .001]. A higher proportion of case mothers reported a traumatic experience [χ^2 (1, n = 316) = 16.1, p < = .001]. When women who reported never experiencing any trauma are removed, PTSD was still higher in the case mothers [53% vs. 33%, χ^2 (1, n = 176) = 5.4, p = .02]. Almost half of case mothers reported at least one Axis I psychiatric disorder, χ^2 (1, n = 316) = 15.5, p = .001.

Drug Abuse/Dependence. Significantly more homeless women had ever used drugs, χ^2 (1, n = 311) = 20.2, p = .001 (Table IV). Only 10% of the homeless drug users first became homeless at an age younger than the reported age of first drug usage. These ten percent were first homeless at younger ages than the other 90% of homeless drug users (18.8 ± 3.5 vs. 25.9 ± 5.7), t (21.6) = 6.8, p < .001. Thirty-seven percent of case mothers (51.4% of case drug users) reported at least one symptom of drug abuse or dependence compared to 18% of control mothers (38.5% of control drug users), χ^2 (1, n = 311) = 12.6, p = .001. Almost all of the positive diagnoses (N = 61, 84.7%) were classified moderate dependence by the DIS/DSM-III-R.

Separating crack/cocaine users from other drug users showed that the rate of drug abuse/dependence was higher among cocaine users and that crack/cocaine use was higher in the homeless sample. Less than a fourth of the other drug users reported abuse or dependence on the drug while two-thirds of the crack/cocaine users reported abuse or dependence on it. Use (χ^2 (1, n = 311) = 18.7, p = .001) and abuse/dependence (χ^2 (1, n =

TABLE III. The Mothers' Childhood and Family History

	CASE N = 202		CONTROL N = 114		TOTAL SAMPLE N = 316	
	N	%	N	%	N	%
Childhood Home						
no father figure	44	21.78	28	24.56	72	22.78
male wage earner	159	78.71	89	78.07	248	78.48
welfare income	60	30.15*	22	19.30	82	26.20
placed in foster or group home	36	17.82*	9	7.89	45	14.24
physical fighting in home	67	33.17	29	25.44	96	30.38
History of Child Abuse						
sexual molestation	68	33.66*	24	21.05	92	29.11
physical abuse	89	44.06	45	39.47	134	42.41
emotional abuse	141	69.80*	66	57.89	207	65.51
any abuse	167	82.67**	77	67.54	244	77.22
Teenage Years						
gave birth before age 17	65	32.34	33	28.95	98	31.11
left home before age 17	54	26.73**	16	14.04	70	22.15
Family history of:						
homelessness	34	16.83	18	15.79	52	16.46
substance abuse	82	40.59	47	41.23	129	40.82
other psychiatric disorder[1]	52	25.74	22	19.30	74	23.42

* p < .05
** p ≤ .01

[1] Specifically, depression, mania or schizophrenia

311) = 13.8, p = .001) of crack/cocaine but not other drugs were both higher in the homeless group compared to the housed (Table IV). Seventeen percent of control drug users reported ever using crack/cocaine compared to 40% of the case drug users. Similar proportions of both samples reported using only other drugs and the rates of abuse/dependence on these drugs were nearly identical for both groups.

Alcoholism and Antisocial Personality (ASP). There was no difference between the two groups in the prevalence of alcohol abuse/dependence whether abuse and dependence were compared separately or combined. A positive diagnosis for alcoholism was positively correlated with all other psychiatric diagnoses in this analysis (specifically ASP, PTSD, Depression, any Axis I disorder, cocaine abuse/dependence and other drug abuse/

TABLE IV. Rates of DIS/DSM-IIIR Psychiatric Diagnoses

	CASE N = 202		CONTROL N = 114		TOTAL SAMPLE N = 316	
	N	%	N	%	N	%
Somatization	1	0.50	0	–	1	0.32
Panic Disorder	7	3.47	4	3.51	11	3.48
Generalized Anxiety	13	6.47	3	2.63	16	5.06
Post-Traumatic Stress Disorder	70	34.83***	15	13.51	85	27.24
Reported Any Trauma	132	65.35***	48	42.11	180	56.96
Major Depression	46	22.77**	12	10.53	58	18.35
Dysthymia	18	8.91	5	4.39	23	7.28
Mania	5	2.48	1	0.88	6	1.90
Schizophrenia	6	2.97	1	0.88	7	2.22
ANY AXIS I DISORDER	91	45.05***	26	22.81	117	37.02
Alcohol Abuse/Dependence	41	20.71	20	17.86	61	19.68
Drug Abuse/Dependence	58	29.29***	14	12.39	72	23.15
Cannabis	24	12.12	8	7.08	32	10.29
Cocaine/Crack	39	19.70***	5	4.42	44	14.15
PCP	8	4.04	1	0.89	9	2.89
Any Drug Except Cocaine/Crack	19	9.60	9	7.96	28	9.00
Antisocial Personality	24	12.63*	6	5.26	30	9.87
ANY LIFETIME DIAGNOSIS	118	58.42***	43	37.72	161	50.95
ANY DRUG USE	142	71.72***	52	46.02	194	62.38
Any Crack/Cocaine Use	57	28.79***	9	7.96	66	21.22
Only non-cocaine drug use	85	42.93	43	38.05	128	41.16

* $p < .05$
** $p \leq .01$
*** $p = .001$

dependence) and also with cocaine use, leaving home before age 17, and all three child abuse variables. Although significantly more ASP was diagnosed in the case mothers $\chi^2 (1, n = 304) = 4.3, p = .04$ (Table IV), the diagnosis of ASP was not selected by the SAS stepwise procedure and was dropped from the multivariate analysis. It was associated with several other variables in the analysis: childhood molestation; foster, group or detention home placement; leaving home before age 17; experiencing trauma and a positive PTSD diagnosis; alcoholism; and cocaine abuse/dependence.

Multivariate Model. Twenty-five measurements were entered into a stepwise logistic regression model to identify those most strongly related to homelessness for St. Louis women. Nine demographic variables were found to discriminate between the two groups of women at the bivariate level (number of biological children, age first pregnant, single parenthood status, never legally married, currently married, completed high school or GED, years of education, school dropout, and paid employment) as were six significant childhood variables (Table III) and six lifetime psychiatric diagnosis variables (PTSD, depression, any Axis I disorder, number of Axis I disorders, ASP and cocaine dependence). In addition, number of biological fathers of the children, average K-BIT score, any cocaine use and reports of trauma were also entered into the stepwise regression procedure. The multivariate model selected is shown in Table V. Eleven cases and five controls could not be utilized in the final multivariate model because of missing data. The most significant risk factors selected were number of children, cocaine use, being a single parent, a diagnosis of PTSD and dropping out of school. Being married and demonstrating average cognitive skills decreased the odds of becoming homeless.

DISCUSSION

Study Strengths and Limitations. A major strength of this study was the use of a comparison group of housed poor mothers with dependent children randomly selected from neighborhoods where the homeless mothers had lived just prior to their enlistment in the epidemiologic study. Most of the other published studies on homeless mothers with dependent children have utilized convenience samples or normative population information for comparison (Breakey et al., 1989; D'Ercole & Struening, 1990; Zima, Wells, Benjamin, & Duan, in press). Very few of the other studies have obtained mental health diagnostic information on both the case and comparison groups of mothers (Goodman, 1991b; Weitzman, Knickman, & Shinn, 1992; Wood, Valdez, Hayashi, & Shen, 1990). None of the other studies include information on cognitive abilities of either case or control groups of mothers. In addition, this study was completed on a large sample with a high completion rate (over 80%) and a refusal rate of only two percent.

Comparison with Other Studies. The demographic characteristics of the homeless and the housed women in this study, including mean maternal age, number of children in the household and level of the mother's formal education, are generally consistent with those of other studies that analyzed a sample of homeless mothers and a comparison group of housed mothers. In addition, the homeless women in this study were less likely to be married and more likely to be single-parent heads-of-household than the housed mothers. Although this could be interpreted as indicating lack of social support, findings in response to formal questions regarding per-

TABLE V. Multivariate Model of Homelessness in Women

LOGISTIC REGRESSION MODEL	ODDS RATIO	95% C.I.	p
1. Number of Children	1.41	1.15-1.71	0.0008
2. Used Crack or Cocaine	4.14	1.77-9.68	0.001
3. Single Parent Household	2.21	1.27-3.87	0.005
4. Legally Married	0.34	0.14-0.80	0.01
5. Post-Traumatic Stress Disorder	2.38	1.17-4.84	0.02
6. Dropped Out of School	1.87	1.06-3.29	0.03
7. Average or Above Average KBIT Score	0.56	0.31-0.99	0.05

ception of social supports were similar to those reported by Goodman (1991b) as well as Shinn and colleagues (1991).

Rates of reported childhood physical abuse are similar to those found by Goodman (1991a) when taking into account her moderately and severely abused groups, but much lower if Goodman's minimally abused group is considered. Rates of reported childhood sexual abuse are much lower in the present sample than in Goodman's sample, yet interestingly, in this study, a significant difference was still found at the bivariate level ($p < 0.05$) between case and control mothers in their reports of childhood sexual molestation.

Rates of psychiatric diagnoses among homeless women are higher in the present study than in the one other study with a comparison group that reports diagnostic rates (Bassuk & Rosenberg, 1988). It is not clear if this is due to use of a structured interview, such as the DIS, for diagnostic information. Currently, there is disagreement in the literature whether structured interviews are prone to yield higher rates of mental illness or whether they tend to underrecognize severe mental illness, particularly in this population (Fischer, Shapiro, Breakey, Anthony, & Kramer, 1986).

Lastly, it is worth noting that the sample of homeless women with dependent children has occasionally been defined in the literature as women who physically have their children with them at the time they are in the shelter (Johnson & Kreuger, 1989). For the present study, any homeless woman who reported having dependent children, whether or not they were with her at the time of homelessness, was included in the case sample.

Implications for Intervention/Prevention. The final results of this analysis provide further understanding of characteristics that distinguish homeless mothers from similar housed women. From the multivariate model we have learned that having more children at an earlier age, dropping out of high school, scoring poorly on a standardized test of cognitive skills, having a diagnosis of PTSD, and using crack/cocaine are strongly associated with the risk of experiencing homelessness. These factors could be interpreted as "behaviors" of the women in this study. In addition, the homeless women in this study were less likely to be married and more likely to be single-parent heads-of-household, factors which could be interpreted as "life circumstances," although potentially related to the previously mentioned behaviors.

We make this distinction after observing which factors remained significant in moving from the bivariate level of analysis to the multivariate model. We noted some factors that could be interpreted as "behaviors" seemed to retain significance while other factors which could be interpreted as "life circumstances" did not. For example, the mother's age at the time of the first live childbirth, a diagnosis of depression, or any history of childhood abuse or neglect could be thought of as "life circumstances." All of these factors were significant at the bivariate level, but not in the multivariate model. Instead, factors which reflected "behaviors" on the part of the mother more frequently remained significant.

If this interpretation of the findings has merit, several implications for intervention and/or prevention of homelessness become apparent. As mental health practitioners know, many behaviors can be changed before they have an impact on life circumstances. Furthermore, several of the behaviors identified in this study as characteristics of homeless women with dependent children can be identified as occurring in late childhood or early adolescence. If health care providers and educators would place renewed emphasis on elementary and high school programs targeting high-risk behaviors such as teenage pregnancy, drug use, and dropping out, a secondary benefit of preventing homelessness might be achieved.

For homeless women whose behaviors have already had an impact on their life circumstances, the solution requires intervention at a different level. If these women are to exit homelessness and avoid future episodes of homelessness, comprehensive mental health services for substance abuse and psychological problems are needed. Educational opportunities addressing pre-employment, parenting, and day-to-day living skills will be required (Nunez, 1994), along with extensive socioeconomic supports that include access to low income housing and day care services. (Johnson & Kreuger, 1989; Rog, Holupka, & McCombs-Thornton, 1996; Weinreb & Buckner, 1993).

The programs necessary to prevent homelessness or to bring families out of homelessness may not be easily funded. Impact studies, cost-benefit analyses, and program evaluations are needed. Researchers need to continue to identify antecedents and consequences of homelessness in order to develop cost effective interventions at appropriate times, as well as to show the positive effects of programs that are currently in place. Homelessness is a complex phenomenon, the causes and correlates of which continue to be defined. Intervention and prevention policies and programs must reflect this complexity and be put in place at an early enough time to be effective.

REFERENCES

American Psychiatric Association. (1987). *American Psychiatric Association: Diagnostic and Statistical Manual of Mental Disorders, Third Edition, Revised.* Washington, DC: American Psychiatric Association.

Bassuk, E.L., & Rosenberg, L. (1988). Why does family homelessness occur? A case-control study. *American Journal of Public Health, 78,* 783-788.

Breakey, W.R., Fischer, P.J., Kramer, M., Nestadt, G., Romanoski, A.J., Ross, A. (1989). Health and mental health problems of homeless men and women in Baltimore. *The Journal of the American Medical Association, 262,* 1352-1357.

Browne, A. (1993). Family violence and homelessness: The relevance of trauma histories in the lives of homeless women. *American Journal of Orthopsychiatry, 63,* 370-383.

D'Ercole, A., & Struening, E. (1990). Victimization among homeless women: Implications for service delivery. *Journal of Community Psychology, 18,* 141-152.

Fischer, P.J., Shapiro, S., Breakey, W.R., Anthony, J.C., & Kramer, M. (1986). Mental health and social characteristics of the homeless: A survey of mission users. *American Journal of Public Health, 76,* 519-524.

Fleiss, J.L., Williams, J.B.W., & Dubro, A.F. (1986). The logistic regression analysis of psychiatric data. *Journal of Psychiatric Research, 20,* 195-209.

Goodman, L.A. (1991a). The prevalence of abuse among homeless and housed poor mothers: A comparison study. *American Journal of Orthopsychiatry, 61,* 489-500.

Goodman, L.A. (1991b). The relationship between social support and family homelessness: A comparison study of homeless and housed mothers. *Journal of Community Psychology, 19,* 321-331.

Goodman, L.A., Dutton, M.A., & Harris, M. (1995). Episodically homeless women with serious mental illness: Prevalence of physical and sexual assault. *American Journal of Orthopsychiatry, 65,* 468-478.

Hausman, B., & Hammen, C. (1993). Parenting in homeless families: The double crises. *American Journal of Orthopsychiatry, 63,* 358-369.

Johnson, A., & Kreuger, L. (1989). Toward a better understanding of homeless women. *Social Work,* 537-540.

Johnson, A.K. (1988). *Homelessness in America: A historical and contemporary assessment.* St. Louis, MO: Washington University.

Kaufman, A.S., & Kaufman, N.L. (1990). *Kaufman brief intelligence test (KBIT).* Circle Pines, MN: American Guidance Service.

Koegel, P., Melamid, E., & Burnam, M.A. (1995). Childhood risk factors for homelessness among homeless adults. *American Journal of Public Health, 856,* 1642-1649.

National Coalition for the Homeless. (1992). *Over the edge: Homeless families and the welfare system.* Washington, D.C. National Coalition for the Homeless.

Nunez, R.D. (1994). *Hopes, Dreams, & Promises: The Future of Homeless Children in America.* New York, NY: Institute for Children and Poverty.

Robertson, M.J. (1991). Homeless women with children: The role of alcohol and other drug abuse. *American Psychologist, 46,* 1198-1204.

Robins, L.N., Helzer, J.E., Croughan, J., Williams, J.B.W., & Spitzer, R.L. (1981). *NIMH Diagnostic Interview Schedule: Version III (May 1981).* National Institute of Mental Health.

Robins, L.N., & Regier, D.A. (1991). *Psychiatric Disorders in America: The Epidemiologic Catchment Area Study.* New York, NY: The Free Press.

Rog, D.J., Holupka, S., & McCombs-Thornton, K.L. (1996). Implementation of the homeless families program: 1. Service models and preliminary outcomes. *American Journal of Orthopsychiatry, 65,* 502-513.

SAS Institute, I. (1996). *SAS User's Guides.* Cary, NC: SAS Institute, Inc.

Shinn, M., Knickman, J.R., & Weitzman, B.C. (1991). Social relationships and vulnerability to becoming homeless among poor families. *American Psychologist, 46,* 1180-1187.

Smith, E.M., North, C.S., & Spitznagel, E.L. (1992). A systematic study of mental illness, substance abuse, and treatment in 600 homeless men. *Annals of Clinical Psychiatry, 4,* 111-120.

Waxman, L. (1994). *A status report on hunger and homelessness in America's cities.* Washington, DC: United States Conference of Mayors.

Weinreb, L., & Buckner, J.C. (1993). Homeless families: Program responses and public policies. *American Journal of Orthopsychiatry, 63,* 400-409.

Weitzman, B.C., Knickman, J.R., & Shinn, M. (1992). Predictors of shelter use among low-income families: Psychiatric history, substance abuse and victimization. *American Journal of Public Health, 82,* 1547-1550.

Wood, D., Valdez, R.B., Hayashi, T., & Shen, A. (1990). Homeless and housed families in Los Angeles: A study comparing demographic, economic, and family function characteristics. *American Journal of Public Health, 80,* 1049-1052.

Zima, B.T., Wells, K.B., Benjamin, B., & Duan, N. (In press). Mental health problems among homeless mothers: Relationship to service use and child mental health problems. *Archives of General Psychiatry.*

Preventing Relapse Among Crack-Using Homeless Women with Children: Building Bridges to the Community

Gerald J. Stahler
Temple University
Rev. Catherine Godboldte
Bridges to the Community
Thomas E. Shipley, Jr.
Temple University
Irving W. Shandler
Diagnostic and Rehabilitation Center
Lucille Ijoy
Bridges to the Community
Anne Weinberg
Temple University
Nancy Harrison-Horn
Diagnostic and Rehabilitation Center
Colita Nichols
Temple University
Lori Simons
Temple University
Linda Koszowski
Diagnostic and Rehabilitation Center

The authors acknowledge the assistance of Denise Snead and Grace Godwin in the collection of information for this manuscript.

Support for this project was partially provided by the Center for Substance Abuse Treatment, Department of Health and Human Services, Grant No. 1HD8 TI0000963.

[Haworth co-indexing entry note]: "Preventing Relapse Among Crack-Using Homeless Women with Children: Building Bridges to the Community." Stahler, Gerald J. et al. Co-published simultaneously in *Journal of Prevention & Intervention in the Community* (The Haworth Press, Inc.) Vol. 15, No. 2, 1997, pp. 53-66; and: *Diversity Within the Homeless Population: Implications for Intervention* (ed: Elizabeth M. Smith, and Joseph R. Ferrari) The Haworth Press, Inc., 1997, pp. 53-66. Single or multiple copies of this article are available for a fee from The Haworth Document Delivery Service [1-800-342-9678, 9:00 a.m. - 5:00 p.m. (EST). E-mail address: getinfo@haworth.com].

INTRODUCTION

Crack cocaine has had a particularly adverse effect on the inner-city African-American communities throughout the United States, and has been especially prevalent among the homeless in many cities (Stahler & Cohen, 1995). There is some evidence to suggest that women have been especially affected by this substance with higher rates of dependence, but lower rates of treatment entry and retention, than men (Inciardi, Lockwood, & Poettiger, 1993; Wallace, 1991; Washton & Gold, 1987).

For those who enter drug treatment, relapse rates during and after program engagement tend to be high for those who are addicted to crack cocaine (Wallace, 1991). Preventing relapse among clients who are addicted to crack cocaine and who are also homeless is particularly problematic because of the multitude of needs that homeless individuals have. For example, homeless individuals not only are residentially unstable, they also tend to have poor economic and employment possibilities, and often lack personal supports and linkages with family, friends, and community institutions (Robertson, Zlotnick, Westerfelt, 1993; Stahler, 1995b). In many cases they are difficult to treat because they have problems in establishing relationships with treatment providers, are extremely mobile (which can preclude continuity of care), and are frequently viewed by service providers as not being "desirable" or "good" patients (Breakey, 1987).

Although there have been relatively few drug treatment programs designed especially to serve the special needs of the homeless (for some notable exceptions see Conrad et al., 1993; Stahler, 1995; Argeriou & McCarty, 1990), even fewer have been targeted to homeless *women* with children (Elder et al., 1994; Smith, North, & Fox, 1995; Robertson, 1991). Many of these women come from alcoholic or addictive families of origin; experienced early and continuing physical, emotional and sexual abuse; suffer from sexually transmitted diseases including HIV; experience depression; have endured racial discrimination; and tend to have little chance of obtaining long-term, safe, independent, and affordable housing. Unfortunately, as Smith, North, and Fox (1995) note, very little is known about how to effectively provide substance abuse treatment for homeless women.

This paper will describe an innovative treatment and aftercare program for urban homeless crack addicted women with children. It involves a partnership between a residential treatment facility and a coalition of African-American church congregations that was recently initiated and is currently being evaluated. The program is designed to prevent relapse and maintain sobriety by linking inpatient treatment to a culturally-sensitive, community-based intervention that involves congregants from the African-American spiritual community. The target population for this program are women with children under six years old who are either homeless or residentially unstable, and who are addicted to crack cocaine.

This paper will first present the background and design of the program, then describe the characteristics of the clients, and finally report on some of the preliminary treatment engagement data.

PROGRAM NEED

Unfortunately, most treatment programs (with some exceptions) have not been designed for the specific needs of women, nor have they been developed with a sensitivity to the cultural backgrounds of their clients (Finkelstein, 1994; Rowe & Grills, 1993). Many women who need treatment for substance use have children who cannot be accommodated within the treatment program. As a result, many do not enter treatment because they do not want to place their children in foster care or they fear that they may lose custody of their children. For example, one study conducted in a Methadone clinic found that 91% of the female clients were mothers, and 63% of them had lost custody of at least one child (Pivnick et al., 1991). As Finkelstein (1994) states,

> Very few programs . . . offer women the opportunity to have their children with them while they are in residential treatment. . . . [This] reflects the belief of many in the addictions field that women should be treated separately from their children. . . . [This] reflects a lack of understanding of access issues, of maternal and child health issues, and of the fact that true recovery for a mother usually works only when it includes her children. (p. 9)

Women substance users, in comparison to men, tend to have more instability in their families of origin, lower self esteem, and a history of sexual abuse (Institute of Medicine, 1990; Weiner, Wallen, & Zankowski, 1990). They also may have less social support for quitting drugs than men (Boyd & Mieczkowski, 1990; Inciardi, Lockwood, & Pottieger, 1993). Homeless crack addicted women are particularly at risk for relapse because of their lack of residential stability; the possibility of return to dysfunctional, abusive families of origin or mates; poor job skills and employment histories; limited parenting, household management, coping, and social skills; and because they often lack adequate social support and bonds to the community and neighborhood (Bassuk, Rubin, & Lauriat, 1986; Comfort, Shipley, White, Griffith, & Shandler, 1990; Dawkins, 1988; Penn et al., 1993).

In addition to the relative paucity of gender-relevant programs, there is frequently an insufficient sensitivity or relevance to clients' culture (see Zweben, 1993). Culturally relevant and sensitive treatment approaches have been increasingly advocated in the literature in recognition of the importance of these factors to the accessibility, acceptance, engagement, and success of interventions for various ethnic and racial populations.

BACKGROUND

In an attempt to meet the treatment needs of homeless crack addicted women with children, the Diagnostic Rehabilitation Center of Philadelphia (DRC), in collaboration with an organization from the African-American spiritual community called "Bridges to the Community," developed a residential and aftercare program that was designed specifically for the needs of homeless crack addicted women with children. DRC opened Hutchinson Place in 1988 as part of a National Institute of Alcohol Abuse and Alcoholism (NIAAA) demonstration program, the first transitional living facility in Philadelphia designed specifically to accommodate homeless drug- and alcohol-addicted pregnant or parenting women and their pre-school children (see Comfort et al., 1990; Shandler et al., 1991). Indeed, the present program represents an evolution of program development for homeless substance abusers that dates back to the era of the redevelopment of skid row slums in American cities described in Blumberg, Shipley, and Shandler (1973) and Blumberg, Shipley, and Barsky (1978). DRC was established in 1963 as a private, non-profit agency in conjunction with Temple University, the Greater Philadelphia Movement (a progressive civic association initiated by the business community), and the City of Philadelphia to provide comprehensive services for substance abusers. It is an independent, free-standing service agency that initially provided services to Skid Row alcoholics, and more recently to the homeless and those in the lower socioeconomic strata of society. "Bridges to the Community" is an organization formed by the Reverend Dr. Catherine Godbolte, a Philadelphia minister, for the purpose of the present project.

In our more recent work with the homeless, especially African-American families, it was clear that important cultural resources reside in the community that can help recovering clients recommit to more prosocial ideals and values. With the support from a demonstration grant from the Center for Substance Abuse Treatment, DRC initiated the present program which involved changing Hutchinson Place from a transitional facility into an inpatient residence; adding a community-based culturally relevant aftercare relapse prevention program which emphasizes new community ties and involvement; and providing an on-site Head Start program for the children.

PROGRAM DESCRIPTION

Program Assumptions. The design of the program was based on a number of findings from the research literature as well as DRC's past experience in providing services to this population. The most extensive research on interventions for homeless substance abusers emerged from the recent NIAAA multisite Homeless Research Demonstration Program that provided funding to local sites to develop and rigorously evaluate innovative programs for homeless substance abusers in various cities throughout the nation (see Conrad, Hultman, & Lyons, 1993; Orwin et al., 1995; Stahler & Cohen, 1995; Stahler, 1995b). From this research, a number of programmatic suggestions and issues have emerged (Stahler, 1995a; Stahler, 1995b):

- Programs that serve homeless substance abusers should not only focus on the client's addiction but need to aggressively address such living needs as housing, income support, and employment in order to sustain recovery.
- Dropout rates are extremely high for this population regardless of type of intervention. However, programs can reduce dropout through various programmatic strategies (Orwin et al., 1995; Stahler et al., 1993).
- Positive treatment outcomes seem to decline over time suggesting the need for longer-term, continuous interventions (see Mumme, 1991).
- Aftercare needs to address not only the maintenance of sobriety but also the social isolation, tangible needs, and alienation from the client's community.

In addition, as some of the authors have advocated elsewhere (Penn et al., 1993), it is essential to:

- nurture the client's sense of hope (positive expectancy);
- reintegrate the homeless client and her children with her community;

- strengthen and build upon the indigenous resources of the community to further support the woman after she has left the treatment setting;
- provide comprehensive interventions that are sensitive and relevant to the client's culture, even though, as Sue and his colleagues (Sue & Zane, 1987; Sue, Zane, & Young, 1994) have noted, it is often difficult to translate cultural relevance, competence, and sensitivity into programmatic activities;
- help clients re-establish their bonds to their spiritual community, one of the most significant institutions within the African-American community.

The church has traditionally provided refuge, solace, a sense of identity and mission, and a viable community and framework for living (Higginbotham, 1993). This has been particularly true in the African-American community, where the church has been an anchor of culture and the family (Gibbs, 1989). The "Bridges" program represents an effort to utilize this institution to promote and sustain culturally-relevant healing and recovery from addiction, and facilitate a reintegration of clients into their community after they have completed residential treatment.

Program Model. Based on these programmatic considerations, DRC and "Bridges" developed the following treatment intervention:

> The program consists of approximately six to nine months of residential care at Hutchinson Place followed by aftercare that includes outpatient counseling and the "Bridges to the Community" program.

Residential Treatment. Hutchinson Place is a free-standing, comprehensive inpatient rehabilitation program for women and their children where all treatment services are provided on-site. Located in North Philadelphia and operated by DRC, it has a capacity for 20 women and 40 children. The program consists of four distinct phases of treatment. During the "Freshman" phase, clients go through a one month "blackout" period devoted to stabilizing, evaluating, and preparing the client for treatment. Clients do not leave the facility during this time since it is believed that it is crucial to remove substance abusers from their normal environment and to eliminate the distractions and complications of daily life in order to focus exclusively on the task of recovery. Medically-supervised detoxification services are available on-site for those who need it. Case managers assist women in accessing resources for which they are eligible, such as Food Stamps, WIC, and other forms of assistance.

During the "Sophomore" phase, which lasts approximately two

months, client families become more deeply involved in their treatment, and receive intensive education on addiction, participate in Alcoholics Anonymous (AA) and Narcotics Anonymous (NA), receive daily individual and group counseling, and attend specialized structured training groups in such areas as anger, assertiveness, relationships, parenting skills, women's health, sexual orientation, coping skills, and relapse prevention. Physical fitness/stress management training is also offered during this phase. Case managers help women learn to prepare personal and household budgets, open bank accounts, master the principles of good nutrition, and develop workable "safety plans" in situations of ongoing domestic violence or sexual abuse. Children attend an onsite Head Start program, one of the first in the nation to be located within a women's drug treatment facility. A developmental clinical psychologist evaluates children for developmental delays or behavioral, educational, emotional, or cognitive problems and strengths. Individualized treatment plans are then developed for children as needed. It is during this phase that clients become introduced to the "Bridges" component; begin to meet with their mentors, or "Big Sisters"; and start to participate in the "Bridges" on-site activities which will be described later.

The "Junior" phase of treatment continues for the next two to four months, and involves a continuation of activities described above and the beginning of family therapy. Pre-vocational and vocational training may be provided at this time as appropriate, and a housing assessment and referral process is undertaken. During this phase, clients are expected to demonstrate both serious investment and significant progress in the therapeutic process, and advance in the application of their parenting and life skills.

In the "Senior" phase of the inpatient treatment which occurs during the last two months of the program, emphasis is placed on preparation for the transition from the structured inpatient environment back to the community. An aggressive search for housing is implemented, counseling and relapse prevention is intensified, and linkages to community support services are firmed up. Departure from Hutchinson place is viewed as a process rather than a single event, and intense planning for continuing care begins no less than six weeks prior to the woman's expected discharge date. Women are assigned to a special "Phase Out" group to alleviate the fears of leaving. They also become "Big Sisters" to new clients and their children.

Aftercare. Aftercare appears to be critical for the long-term continuation of gains obtained in treatment (Mumme, 1991; Stahler, Shipley, Bartelt, & DuCette, 1995). This component consists of continuing outpatient counseling for approximately six to nine months after leaving Hutchinson Place, involvement in AA and NA, continuation in the "Bridges" program, and a monthly "alumnae" group. After completing one year of outpatient counseling, there is a graduation ceremony that involves a certificate; the presentation of flowers to the women from their counselors; and an opportunity for the Hutchinson Place staff, the woman's family, and friends to speak about the women's achievement.

Although "Bridges" is an aftercare program, clients become involved in it while they are still in residence at Hutchinson Place. This program consists of two major components: interactions with a Community Anchor Person (CAP), and group activities including workshops, training sessions, and cultural and recreational endeavors.

Community Anchor Persons (CAPs). Approximately 25 African-American women from various churches and other faith communities have been enlisted and trained to be CAPs. These trained women provide clients with individual and group fellowship and companionship, sponsorship and mentoring, as well as assistance with housing, child care, and other concerns. The goal is to offset the alienation and social isolation of the recovering woman and her family, particularly when the risk of relapse is greatest (after leaving the residential treatment facility), and to facilitate her transition back into the community.

During the first year of operation, the CAPs have ranged in age from 28 to 62, and work as teachers, nurses, ministers, and homemakers. They vary in their educational background from high school diplomas to graduate degrees, and were recommended to the program by their pastors. Three CAPs are women in recovery. Each CAP is paid a monthly stipend for a commitment of a minimum of 20 hours per month to the program. They attend monthly training workshops on such topics as communication skills, building self-esteem, stages of development, community activism, parenting responsibilities, cultural heritage, home and money management, healthy living, and spiritual activities.

Each client is matched with a CAP on an individual basis by the "Bridges" program director according to the client's preferred church or spiritual affiliation, personality, and geographic location. Initially, each CAP was matched to a client during the "senior" phase of treatment, approximately six weeks before she was scheduled to graduate from Hutchinson Place. However, more recently, CAPs are being matched to clients approximately one month after admission so as to form a closer relationship during most of the client's stay in Hutchinson Place.

Each CAP and client communicate daily either by phone or in person while at Hutchinson Place as well as after the client graduates from the program. The clients also understand that they may call on their CAP any time they feel they need to talk to them. After the client leaves Hutchinson

Place, the CAP accompanies and introduces her to families in the chosen church community. The CAP and the client also participate in bi-weekly social events usually involving child-related activities, and attend various church and social functions together. Outings have included gospel concerts, plays, and religious revivals. CAPs help link the client to both the formal and informal resources of the community to help clients with finding housing as well as with therapeutic and recreational activities.

Important functions of the CAP are to form a supportive relationship with the client, act as a mentor and a friend, and assist her and her children in whatever way she can. For example, CAPs have been very active in helping clients secure housing and to obtain furniture and other household goods by securing donations from their various church communities. At present, there is no defined termination point when the CAP ceases meeting with her "Little Sister."

Group Activities. In addition to the monthly training sessions mentioned above for the CAPs to which clients who have graduated are also invited, "Bridges" provides two types of weekly workshops at Hutchinson Place. Each Friday morning clients in Hutchinson Place attend workshops that usually involve music and dance. This is followed by a weekly class that involves spiritual enlightenment as well as Life Skills training. Classes have dealt with Bible Study as well as such Life Skills as values clarification, healthy relationships, decision-making, child-rearing skills, domestic violence, and cultural learning and pride. A critical aspect of these workshops is that they are culturally relevant. There is always an emphasis on African culture and the African spiritual worldview. Cultural celebrations and the remembrance of one's cultural heritage is emphasized in the workshops because it is believed that "grounding" or "centering" an individual in her cultural identity will further sustain her recovery. This perspective tends to unify the secular with the sacred, and incorporates certain spiritual rituals on a daily basis. For example, each session is opened and closed with invocation, prayer, and song. Clients are encouraged to engage in daily devotional meditation exercises; and to maintain a daily diary of their thoughts, feelings, and experiences. Some workshops have focused on certain cultural events such as the African-American holiday Kwanzaa, while others have consisted of discussions of books that deal with the African-American experience. In fact, reading and discussion has proven to be so popular among the clients that "Bridges" has initiated a mobile book lending library. Whenever possible, the clients' children are also involved in activities, and the women are encouraged to read to them.

CLIENT CHARACTERISTICS AND OUTCOMES

Although Hutchinson Place has been in operation as a transitional residence since 1988, it added the "Bridges" program in October, 1994, became a licensed inpatient facility in June, 1995, and began matching clients with CAPs in May, 1995. In this section of the paper, we will describe some of the client characteristics of those who have thus far been admitted to the program, and present some preliminary information on outcomes.

After approximately one year of full operation, a total of 36 women have received baseline interviews. Table 1 displays some of the demographic characteristics and drug use information concerning the clients. In general, the women served have for the most part been young, never married, African-American, crack-addicted mothers with several children. Slightly less than half have completed high school, and very few have had any college education. The majority have had prior treatment for drugs or alcohol, and most have used drugs for a number of years. More than 90% have smoked crack for more than one year, with the average age of initiation of cocaine use being 19 years old. On average, the clients report having started smoking tobacco at age 11, marijuana at age 13, and drinking alcohol at age 15. Most have come from homes where alcohol was used frequently within their family of origin.

About one third of the clients admit to trading sex for drugs, and slightly more than one quarter report that they had earned money as prostitutes. Slightly less than half (46%) report being domestically abused, and 20% have been victims of rape. These data are probably an underestimate because of the sensitivity of the issue and because the data are collected very shortly after admission to the program. Finally, about 25% of the clients report being literally homeless for at least one month during the past year with the average duration being two months. However, most clients have had substantial residential instability including doubling up in friends' or relatives' houses. Only a quarter of the clients have spent the majority of the prior six months in their own apartment or home.

Although it is early to report on any outcome data, the initial results seem to be promising in terms of graduation rates and relapse. Over the past six years at Hutchinson Place, prior to the full implementation of the current project, graduation rates averaged 29%, with about two thirds of the clients either dropping out or being discharged for various reasons such as relapse or rules violation. Since the full implementation of the present program, the graduation rate (excluding those still in residence) has been averaging approximately 50%. Of the 36 clients who entered the program, 17 have dropped out. Only two of these dropouts had been in the program long enough to have been paired with a CAP. Of the 20 clients

TABLE 1. Client Characteristics

Characteristic	n = 36
Age Mean Range	 30.0 years 20-39 years
Race/Ethnicity African-American Caucasian	 97% 3%
Education Mean Years High School Graduates Some College	 10.9 years (s.d. = 1.9) 47% 8%
Marital Status Single, never married Married Separated Divorced	 81% 6% 11% 3%
Number of Children Mean Range	 3.1 children (s.d. = 1.6) 1-7 children
Primary Drug of Abuse Cocaine (crack) alone Cocaine & Heroin Cocaine & Alcohol	 83% 3% 14%
Prior Drug/Alcohol Treatment % with Prior Treatment Mean No. Prior Treatments	 75% 2.6 times (s.d. = 1.6)

who have been paired with CAPs, two dropped out of Hutchinson prior to graduation (as just mentioned), one relapsed after graduation, and the remaining 17 clients graduated from Hutchinson Place and have maintained sobriety. In addition, all clients reside in independent housing, mostly in houses with rent subsidies, with the exception of one woman who is living with her mother. These data, although promising, must be viewed with caution because of the small numbers, the lack of a comparison or control group, and because these represent only preliminary data after slightly less than one year of full program implementation. Also, most of these clients were paired with "Bridges" CAPs after the period when clients are most likely to drop out and thus probably represent clients who would be expected to have more favorable outcomes.

CONCLUSIONS

In conclusion, we believe that this program holds considerable promise for enabling crack-addicted African-American women with children to become abstinent and maintain their sobriety in the community. The program's strengths involve its cultural relevance, its emphasis on meeting the multiplicity of needs of these women and children, its focus on aftercare and social support, and its focus on reducing her social isolation by helping the client renew her bonds with members of her spiritual community to sustain her recovery after treatment.

While those involved in this project cannot help but feel excited by the potential of the program, the effectiveness of the project needs to be evaluated using a rigorous comparative design. Long-term follow-up assessments need to be conducted to determine how well the women actually maintain their sobriety and how well they become re-integrated into their community. In addition, given the realities of managed care, to what degree can the inpatient part of the intervention be reduced without attenuating its effectiveness? To what degree can this program be replicated in other communities? What impact does the program have on the children of these women? Over the next two years, we hope to learn a great deal more about how best to implement the program as well as to gain more information on the impact of this intervention on the clients. We hope that by combining the professional care system with the indigenous resources of the community, that treatment can be humanized, made culturally relevant, and better meet the needs of addicted women with children.

REFERENCES

Argeriou, M., & McCarty, D. (Eds.). (1990). Treating alcoholism and drug abuse among homeless men and women: Nine community demonstration grants [special issue]. *Alcohol Treatment Quarterly, 7*(1).

Bassuk, E., Rubin, L., & Lauriat, A. (1986). Characteristics of sheltered homeless families. *American Journal of Public Health, 76,* 1097-1101.

Boyd, C.J., & Mieczkowski, T. (1990). Drug use, health, family and social support in 'crack' cocaine users. *Addictive Behaviors, 15,* 481-485.

Breakey W. (1987). Treating the homeless. *Alcohol Health and Research World, 11,* 42-47.

Comfort, M., Shipley, T.E., Jr., White, K., Griffith, E.M., & Shandler, I.W. (1990). Family treatment for homeless alcohol/drug-addicted women and their preschool children, *Alcoholism Treatment Quarterly, 7,* 129-147.

Conrad, K., Hultman, C., Lyons, J. (Eds.). (1993). *Treatment of the chemically dependent homeless: Theory and implementation in fourteen American projects.* New York: The Haworth Press, Inc.

Dawkins, M.P. (1988). Alcoholism prevention and black youth. *Journal of Drug Issues, 18,* 15-20.

Elder, M., Hogue, A., Shipley, T., Jr., & Shandler, I. (1994). A comparison of addictive behaviors between homeless men and women. In R.R. Watson (Ed.), *Drug and Alcohol Abuse Reviews, Vol.5: Addictive Behaviors in Women.* Totowa, NJ: Humana Press.

Finkelstein, N. (1994). Treatment issues for alcohol- and drug-dependent pregnant and parenting women. *Health and Social Work, 19,* 7-15.

Gibbs, J.T. (1989). Black American adolescents. In J.T. Gibbs, L.N. Huang & Associates (Eds.), *Children of color: Psychological interventions with minority youth.* San Francisco: Jossey-Bass.

Higginbotham, E.B. (1993). *Righteous discontent: The women's movement in the black Baptist church.* Cambridge, MA: Harvard University Press.

Inciardi, J.A., Horowitz, R., Pottieger, A.E. (1993). *Street Kids, Street Drugs, Street Crime.* Belmont, CA: Wadsworth Publishing.

Inciardi, J.A., Lockwood, D., Pottieger, A.E. (1993). *Women and crack-cocaine.* New York: Macmillan.

Institute of Medicine. (1990). *Broadening the base of treatment for alcohol problems.* Washington, D.C.: National Academy Press.

Mumme, D. (1991). Aftercare: Its role in primary and secondary recovery of women from alcohol and other drug dependence. *International Journal of the Addictions, 26,* 549-564.

Orwin, R.G., Garrison-Mogren, R., Jacobs, M.L., Sonnefeld, L.J., & Perl, H.I. (1995, August). *Cross-site synthesis of retention analyses from the NIAAA Cooperative Agreement Program for Homeless Persons with Alcohol and Other Drug Problems.* Paper presented at the American Psychological Association annual meeting, New York, NY.

Penn, M., Stahler, G., Shipley, T., Comfort, M., and Weinberg, A. (1993). Returning home: Reintegration of substance abusing African-American mothers. *Contemporary Drug Problems, 20,* 473-497.

Pivnick, A., Mulvihill, M., Jacomson, A., Hsu, M.A., Eric, K., Druker, E. (1991). Reproductive decisions among HIV-infected, drug-using women: The importance of mother-child coresidence. *Medical Anthropology Quarterly, 5,* 153-169.

Robertson, M. (1991). Homeless women with children: The role of alcohol and other drug abuse. *American Psychologist, 46,* 1198-1204.

Robertson M.J., Zlotnick C., Westerfelt A. (1993). Homeless adults: A special population in public alcohol treatment programs. *Contemporary Drug Problems, 20,* 499-520.

Rowe, D., & Grills, C. (1993). African-centered drug treatment: An alternative conceptual paradigm for drug counseling with African-American clients. *Journal of Psychoactive Drugs, 25,* 21-33.

Shandler, I.W., Shipley, T.E., Jr., White, K., Callahan, M., Comfort, M., Richlin, L. (1991). *Families of recovering mothers.* Final report to the National Institute of Alcohol Abuse and Alcoholism on Grant No. 2R18 AA07966-02. Philadelphia: Diagnostic and Rehabilitation Center.

Smith, E.M., North, C.S., Fox, L.W. (1995). Eighteen-month follow-up data on a treatment program for homeless substance abusing mothers. *Journal of Addictive Diseases, 14,* 57-72.

Stahler, G. (Ed.). (1995a). The effectiveness of social interventions for homeless substance abusers [special issue]. *Journal of Addictive Diseases, 14* (4).

Stahler, G. (1995b). Social interventions for homeless substance abusers: Evaluating treatment outcomes. *Journal of Addictive Diseases, 14,* xv-xxvi.

Stahler, G., & Cohen, E. (1995a). Homelessness and substance abuse in the 1990s. *Contemporary Drug Problems, 22,* 169-191.

Stahler, G., & Cohen, E. (Eds.). (1995b). Homelessness and substance abuse in the 1990s: Qualitative studies from service demonstration projects [special issue]. *Contemporary Drug Problems, 22.*

Stahler, G., Shipley, T., Bartelt, D., Westcott, D., Griffith, E., and Shandler, I. (1993). Retention issues in treating homeless polydrug users. *Alcoholism Treatment Quarterly, 10,* 3,4, 201-215.

Stahler, G., Shipley, T., Bartelt, D., & DuCette, J. (1995). Evaluating alternative treatments for homeless substance-abusing men: Outcomes and predictors of success. *Journal of Addictive Diseases, 14,* 151-167.

Sue, S., & Zane, N. (1987). The role of culture and cultural techniques in psychotherapy. *American Psychologist, 42,* 458-462.

Sue, S., Zane, N., & Young, K. (1994). Research on psychotherapy with culturally diverse populations. In A.E. Bergin & S.L. Garfield (Eds.), *Handbook of psychotherapy and behavior change* (4th ed.) (pp. 783-817). New York: John Wiley.

Wallace, B.C. (1991). *Crack cocaine: A practical treatment approach for the chemically dependent.* New York: Brunner/Mazel.

Washton, A.M., & Gold, M.S. (1987). *Cocaine: A clinician's handbook.* New York: Guilford Press.

Weiner, H., Wallen, M., & Zankowski, G. (1990). Culture and social class as intervening variables in relapse prevention with chemically dependent women. *Journal of Psychoactive Drugs, 22,* 239-248.

Zweben, J.E. (Ed.) (1993). Culturally relevant substance abuse treatment [special issue]. *Journal of Psychoactive Drugs, 25* (1).

Case Management in Practice: Lessons from the Evaluation of the RWJ/HUD Homeless Families Program

Debra J. Rog
C. Scott Holupka
Kimberly L. McCombs-Thornton
M. Consuelo Brito
Ralph Hambrick

Vanderbilt Institute for Public Policy Studies
Center for Mental Health Policy

INTRODUCTION

While no one strategy has been used or promulgated either to prevent homelessness among families or to help families rise out of it, case management has been among the most common strategies used and promoted (Helvie and Alexy, 1992; MDS Associates, 1993; Weitzman and Berry,

The authors would like to thank the HFP project directors and the National Program Office for their support in this effort, and the case managers across the sites for their assistance and insights. The views expressed, however, are the authors' own and do not necessarily represent the views of the Foundation.

This research was supported by a grant from The Robert Wood Johnson Foundation.

[Haworth co-indexing entry note]: "Case Management in Practice: Lessons from the Evaluation of the RWJ/HUD Homeless Families Program." Rog, Debra J. et al. Co-published simultaneously in *Journal of Prevention & Intervention in the Community* (The Haworth Press, Inc.) Vol. 15, No. 2, 1997, pp. 67-82; and: *Diversity Within the Homeless Population: Implications for Intervention* (ed: Elizabeth M. Smith, and Joseph R. Ferrari) The Haworth Press, Inc., 1997, pp. 67-82. Single or multiple copies of this article are available for a fee from The Haworth Document Delivery Service [1-800-342-9678, 9:00 a.m. - 5:00 p.m. (EST). E-mail address: getinfo@haworth.com].

67

1994). In particular, case management paired with housing, often referred to as supportive housing or services-enriched housing (Friedmutter, 1989), has increasingly become viewed as a promising approach to break the cycle of homelessness for families who have had multiple or chronic experiences with homelessness.

Despite its increasing popularity, there has been little explicit study of case management's operations or effectiveness with families. Much of what is known about case management has come from studies of case management with individuals with mental illnesses, including those who are homeless (e.g., Center for Mental Health Services, 1994; Rife, First, Greenlee, Miller, and Feichter, 1991).

The Homeless Families Program (HFP), a joint initiative of The Robert Wood Johnson Foundation and the U.S. Department of Housing and Urban Development was initiated in August of 1990 in nine sites across the country. A major aspect of the HFP was to combine case management with subsidized housing for multi-problem families living in shelters or in other homeless situations. The HFP, a five year program that officially ended in August of 1995 (with a number of sites continuing beyond this point), was accompanied by an extensive evaluation of both the implementation and outcomes of services-enriched housing.

This article focuses on the implementation of services-enriched housing (the effectiveness of the housing is currently being analyzed). Specifically, this article provides an in-depth look at the structure and operation of case management in the largest demonstration of services-enriched housing for homeless families to date. The lessons learned about the factors that influence the amount and nature of case management delivered should have wide application. Because the HFP involved a range of sites, was modestly funded, and largely drew on existing community resources, the study's implications are more likely to readily transfer to jurisdictions that are interested in trying new approaches but are limited in the resources available.

DESCRIPTION OF THE HOMELESS FAMILIES PROGRAM

Overview

The Homeless Families Program (HFP) was designed to assist nine cities in the development of community-wide systems of comprehensive services for homeless families with multiple and complex problems. Each HFP project received approximately $600,000 over the course of five years. The projects were led by either a city or county public agency, a coalition or task force for the homeless, or another nonprofit provider. The Program had two goals: (1) to demonstrate a model of services-enriched housing for families; and (2) to develop and restructure comprehensive systems of health services, support services, and housing for homeless families who have multiple needs. This article focuses on the services-enriched housing component; interim findings on the systems component are described elsewhere (Rog, Hambrick, Holupka, McCombs, Gilbert, and Brito, 1994).

Families Served. Each HFP project was to provide services-enriched housing to approximately 150 families who were currently homeless (living in shelters or on the streets) and struggling with one or more problems, such as domestic violence, substance abuse, health problems, and others. Over 1500 families across the nine projects received housing and services over the course of the Program; the evaluation tracked 1298 families who entered during the first four years of the Program.

For the most part, HFP families were similar demographically to those families described in other studies of homeless families (Rossi, 1994). Seventy-five percent of the families entered the Program from a shelter, transitional housing, or another homeless situation such as the street, an abandoned building or their car. The remaining twenty-five percent were doubled up with relatives or friends (17%) or had been staying in some other location (e.g., hospital, substance abuse treatment program) (8%). Most had struggled with residential instability for some time.

The majority of families had multiple service needs, including health and mental health, substance abuse, education and training, and others. Rog, McCombs-Thornton, Gilbert-Mongelli, Brito, and Holupka (1995b) describe the characteristics and the constellations of needs of the mothers in the families. Although human capital strengths were significant for over half of the women interviewed (58% had a high school degree or GED; 62% had held a job for a year or longer before intake), all areas of need were pronounced for the population of women served in the Program, especially in comparison to the general population. The most notable indicators were reports of either past or current experience with partner abuse (86%); one or more childhood experiences (e.g., sexual abuse) that indicate risk for future mental health problems (58%); current psychological distress (59%); past hard drug use (49%); and one or more past attempts at suicide (28%). It is important to note that because of the flexibility in the Program selection criteria, there are considerable differences among the sites on most key service need indicators (see Rog et al., 1995b).

Housing and Services. For each family receiving a Section 8 certificate,[1] the HFP lead agency was to obtain services through case management. A guiding hypothesis of the Program was that the "services needed by families generally existed in the community but were not accessible." Therefore, a mechanism such as case management was considered crucial to ensure that services could be accessed for families once they left shelter and moved into their own housing. By helping families link with needed services, the HFP was intended to break the cycle of homelessness, increase the residential stability of families, and in turn, help families ultimately become financially independent.

The Status of Case Management at the Start of HFP. In those sites where case management services were already available for homeless families, they were typically described as "limited" in scope. Most of the case management was provided through shelters, transitional housing, or other homeless service agencies and focused on helping families access services while they were homeless and on facilitating families' transition into housing. Long term case management, defined as following families to permanent housing and continuing for several months or until it is determined to be no longer needed, either did not exist or was in small supply. Therefore, because long-term case management was a key HFP concept, considerable negotiation with providers in the system was needed to ensure that their existing case management services could be restructured to meet the HFP criteria. (This restructuring is described more fully under the network section below.)

In the few sites where long-term case management was available, it was restricted to clients with particular needs such as high risk pregnancy, chronic mental illness, HIV/AIDS, or child abuse. Homeless families, though not the specific target population, often were a subset of the families with these needs. In Oakland, for example, a prenatal substance abuse project provided case management, including a monthly home visit, for up to three years. Some homeless families were able to access services from this program, but homelessness was not a criterion for eligibility.

CASE MANAGEMENT DATA COLLECTION

Key Informant Interviews and Documents. Semi-structured interviews were conducted at several points over the course of the evaluation with a variety of providers, agency officials, and advocates. One focus of the interviews was determining what case management resources were available for homeless families specifically and for families in general. Data were collected longitudinally to monitor changes in the system and HFP's role in these changes. In addition, through interviews with HFP project directors and other key stakeholders, data on the design and intended framework of the case management models in each site were collected. Interviews were supplemented with document reviews.

Case Manager Survey. In 1993, a survey was conducted with all case managers participating in the HFP at that time. The purpose of the survey was to collect background information on the case managers, their organizational involvement, their views on the needs of families, and their philosophy with respect to case management. Individuals who could not complete a questionnaire administered during a site visit were contacted through the mail, and if necessary, by telephone. Up to two mailings and one telephone contact were made to each non-responding case manager to obtain their responses to the survey.

Seventy-nine percent (98 of 125) of the case managers across the nine sites completed a questionnaire. However, four sites had 100% return rates and four sites had over 80%. The one site below 80% (San Francisco) had a disproportionate number of case managers in the total (see Table 1) and thus, its low response rate disproportionally affects the overall response rate.

Case Manager Time Sample. In the third year of the Program (1993), interviews were conducted on-site with a total of 57 case managers. In sites with 7 or fewer case managers, all case managers were interviewed. For sites with larger numbers, a sample of 10 case managers was selected to represent the array of agencies involved in the Program as well as include those case managers who had relatively larger case loads of HFP families.

The interview consisted of a time sample and an assessment of the availability of services in the community. The time sample had three components: yesterday's activities, the past week's activities, and major activities occurring in the prior 30 days. A semi-structured format was used for all three time sample components. The time sample analyses in this article are limited to the "Yesterday" interview in which the respondents were asked to recall the time spent on all job-related activities on the prior work day. Each case manager also was asked to rate how typical the day had been compared to other days and the accuracy of their recall for that time period. Case managers were informed about the nature of the interview at the time they were contacted to participate and were asked to take special note of their activities for the day in question. A sample of interviews were independently coded by two researchers. Questions were flagged and discussed. Coders agreed on activity codes for 95% of the sample's total time at work.

Case Management MIS Records. As part of a larger uniform Manage-

TABLE 1

STRATEGIES	SITES	# OF CM AGENCIES	# OF CMGR	CM SUPERVISOR
Case Management Structure–Early Implementation HFP Project Cities				
Project-Specific	BALT	1	7	x
Case Managers	HOUS	2[a]	5	x
Resource	ATL	1	3	x
Coordinators/Family				
Advocates	NASH[b]	1	4	
	Few Agencies			
	DENV[b]	7[c]	7	
	OAK	2	14	x
	PORT	7	10	x
	Mult. Agencies			
	SF	24	46	x
Case Management Network	SEAT	24	51	x

Note. CM = case management; CMGR = case manager; ATL = Atlanta; BALT = Baltimore; DENV = Denver; HOUS = Houston; NASH = Nashville; OAK = Oakland; PORT = Portland; SF = San Francisco; SEAT = Seattle.
[a]Harris County Hospital District was the lead agency with four case managers; an additional case manager was provided by the Harris County Mental Health and Mental Retardation Authority.
[b]Nashville's project director in the early stages of the Program assumed case managment supervision duties. Denver had intake specialists who provided support to the case managers as well as mental health specialists who assumed a case management coordinator function.
[c]The number of participating agencies dropped to five in the second year of the Program.

ment Information System (MIS) developed by the evaluation team in collaboration with the sites, case managers completed a monthly case management record for each HFP family. For each contact the case manager had with or on behalf of a family, data were recorded on the date of the contact, who was involved, who initiated it, the location or type of contact (e.g., by phone, in person), the length of the contact, and the types of activities conducted during the contact, such as arranging for services or problem solving with the family. Multiple activities could be coded for a single contact.

Analyses in this article are based on person case management contacts for the first 12 months a family was in the HFP. The analyses include those families for whom at least 80% of their first 12 months of case management data were available. (If a family was in the Program less than 12 months, then the criterion was case management data for 80% or more of whatever time period they were in the Program.) Across the sites, sufficient data were available on 75% (n = 974) of the HFP families; in five of the sites, data were available on 80-90% of the families. In one site just over half of the families were excluded due to insufficient data.

A CASE STUDY OF CASE MANAGEMENT

The Intended HFP Approach

Case management was one of the cornerstones of the Homeless Families Program. Although a specific model of case management was not proffered, general direction was provided by the HFP's National Program Office. There was an expectation that case managers would be more than service-brokers, providing families with intensive support when needed. Intensive case management was often referred to as the suggested model and a caseload of 1:20 was offered as a general guide. It was expected that case managers would work individually with families, make frequent home visits, and work with families as long as needed, with the common belief that most families would need at least a year of intervention.

Case Management Configuration

At the start of the HFP, three different general configurations of case management were used in the HFP, as displayed in Table 1: project specific case managers; resource coordinators/family advocates; and case management networks.

Project-Specific. In these sites, the HFP lead agency directly employed full-time or part-time case managers. Case managers were supervised by the HFP project director or another project staff member. RWJ funding was used to support the case management, supplemented with other sources.

Resource Coordinators/Family Advocates. The two projects using either "resource coordinators" or "family advocates" were similar in configuration to those using project-specific case managers. That is, the resource coordinators or family advocates were employed by the lead agency, and HFP funding was used to support their salaries. However, in these two projects, the typical case management role was eschewed and replaced with what was viewed to be a less clinical and traditional approach to working with families. In Atlanta, for example, each resource coordinator lived in her own Section 8 apartment in one of the three complexes where most of the HFP families were clustered, with the intention that she would serve as a grass-roots "community organizer" for the families in her cluster. In Nashville, family advocates considered a major part of their role to be fighting "the system" on behalf of their families in order to get their needs met.

Network. Five of the projects provided case management primarily by leveraging services from existing organizations, such as shelters, transitional housing programs, social services agencies, and other organizations providing family services. Case managers in those organizations, or staff with other responsibilities who took on a case management role, worked with HFP clients as part of their workload.

Two incentives were used to make participation with the HFP worthwhile. One primary incentive was the provision of Section 8 certificates to the clients of the organization providing the case management. A second arrangement involved payment for part or all of the case management services provided to HFP families. For four of the five network sites, however, few funds were provided for the HFP services. Consequently, case managers typically did not work exclusively with HFP families and often had to take these families over and above their current case loads, as well as work with them longer than usual.

Over the course of the HFP, various changes occurred in the configuration of case management. Responding to their own need for more accountability and control, the HFP projects that leveraged case manager networks (especially the larger networks) reduced the number of agencies and number of case managers involved in the HFP and increasingly sought resources to hire one or more project specific case managers directly on staff in the lead agency. Even in the smaller network and non-network projects, changes occurred that affected the case management service delivery (e.g., some agencies discontinued participation).

Case Management Supervision and Coordination

Regardless of case management configuration, each project was led by a full-time project director who worked for the lead agency. In the project-specific and resource coordinator sites, all but one site had either a case management supervisor on staff or a project director who acted as a case management supervisor. Four of the network sites also had case management coordinators or supervisors who worked with the other case management agencies in coordinating cases and data, and on other issues.

Across the sites, case managers reported meeting with their supervisors an average of 2.6 times a month. However, there was quite a range in response. Among the 82 people who responded, eleven percent of the case managers reported never meeting with their supervisor, but nearly half (44%) reported meeting once a week or more. (It is important to note, however, that an additional sixteen case managers either could not or chose not to answer the question.) When asked whether they would like more, less or about the same supervision as now, 65% said the status quo was fine, 31% wanted more, and only four percent indicated a need for less. Those who wanted more supervision commonly said that they wanted more time to talk about specific families and discuss ways of getting necessary information and assistance, while those who were satisfied indicated that these types of needs were being adequately met.

Case Manager Backgrounds

Nearly all of the case managers surveyed were women (91%) and the majority (69%) were in their 30s or 40s. Over eighty-five percent had graduated from college, with nearly half having their Master's degree. In addition, 42% had received other professional certificates or licenses, in areas such as counseling, social work, and nursing. Approximately two thirds of the case managers majored in social work (52%) or psychology (15%). The case managers represented a racial mix, in many respects reflecting both the racial mix of the city itself as well as the population served. The majority of case managers involved in the HFP were new to case management, with 63% working in the field for five years or less. In fact, ten percent of the case managers had been working for one year or less in the role as a case manager at the time of the survey.

Although all 98 individuals surveyed performed case management duties in the HFP, not all were in primary case management roles. Sixty-four percent considered themselves case managers, and an additional 14% were case manager supervisors. Other roles mentioned included shelter staff, public health nurse, and program coordinator. Most (60%) worked for a private not-for-profit agency, with the next largest group (34%) working for a county or city agency. The not-for-profit agencies represented included shelters and transitional housing programs (including those focused on domestic violence), and other types of homeless providers or organizations; health care organizations; and other social services agencies. City and county agencies included health, social services, and homeless service agencies.

Salaries for full-time staff ranged from as low as $10,000-$12,499 to $25,000 and above. Looking at just those survey respondents who considered themselves case managers and who indicated they worked full-time (n = 55), 24% of the case managers reported a gross annual salary of less than $20,000, 37% reported making between $20,000 and $24,999, and 40% reported earning $25,000 or more a year.

The Nature of Case Management

Daily Activities. Analysis of the data from the "Yesterday" time sample interview reveals a wide range of activities for HFP case managers. The range was apparent both in the course of a single case manager's day and across the pool of case managers. In fact, no one activity was reported by all case managers as being performed on the previous work day. In addition, the day appeared to be considered fairly typical, with 80% of the case managers rating it a four or above on a five point scale of typicality.

Most case managers performed the same activities in the course of the day, but often to varying degrees. Seventy-seven percent reported interacting with families some portion of the day. Those who saw clients spent an average of 2 1/2 hours during the day directly with families either in home visits, office visits, etc., though the time ranged from 1/2 hour to 6 1/2 hours.

Other activities that consumed much of the day for most case managers involved phone and paperwork. Almost all case managers reported talking on the phone at some point during the day, usually with clients or to arrange services. They averaged 1 1/2 hours a day on the phone. Over 60% of the case managers stated they spent time on paperwork the previous day for an average of 1 1/2 hours.

Travel was also a common activity. Nearly three quarters reported traveling for their jobs during that day, usually to visit a client at home or to run other errands such as furniture shopping for families or visiting a shelter. Those who traveled typically spent an hour in transit during the day, although the time reported ranged from as little as five minutes to as much as 3 3/4 hours. In addition, in a few sites, notably Houston, families lived in a wide geographic area and thus case managers there spent from 1 1/4 to 1 3/4 hours in the car during the day.

Along with travel, other aspects of their jobs took case managers away from interacting with clients. Those aspects most commonly include face-to-face conversations with co-workers and others regarding their clients and other issues, and formal meetings such as staff meetings. In addition, because HFP case managers often worked in agencies where they perform duties outside of traditional case management, some of their time was spent answering phones for a homeless hot line, providing child care, managing a shelter, waiting at a front desk to process clients for drop-in services, and so on. Although only a quarter of the sample interviewed reported time on non-case management activities, these activities consumed anywhere from five minutes to over half of an individual's work day, with most reporting about an hour on one or more of these activities.

Family Specific Activities. Based on the analysis of families' case management records, the most common case management activity was routine visits from the case manager (an average of 46% of a family's contacts). Other frequently cited activities included arranging or following-up on services (34%), developing service plans (23%), counseling (25%), and problem solving (20%). Other activities, such as responding to crises, advocating for the family, or providing transportation, were less frequently cited (10% less of the contacts reported).

Amount of Case Management Provided

Case-Load Size. When one examines the self-reported case-loads of those survey respondents who considered themselves full time case managers (n = 58), the average case-load was 1:22, close to the suggested HFP guideline of 1:20. However, there was great variation in case-loads, from a low of 2 families (for a recently hired case manager) to a high of 60 families. In fact, 26% of the case managers had a case-load of 30 families or more.

When only the case managers' active case-loads are considered, excluding those families who are considered "inactive" and not currently receiving case management services, the average case-load decreases to 1:19. Furthermore, only 15% of the case managers reported an active case-load of 30 families or more, while slightly more than half (52%) had an active case-load under 20 families.

Intensity of Case Management. The present analysis focused on two measures of case management "intensity" derived from the MIS case management records: the number of hours spent face-to-face with the family during the first 12 months a family was in the HFP; and the number of face-to-face contacts made with the family during the same period.

Each family received an average of 15 case manager contacts and an average of 15 hours of contact during their first 12 months in the HFP (about an hour and one contact a month). However, there was considerable variation in the intensity of case management received across families. For example, while over one quarter (26%) of the families received only 6 or fewer face-to-face contacts during their first year in the HFP, 18% received 24 or more direct contacts (2 contacts a month). At the highest end, three percent of the families had approximately a weekly meeting with the case managers. When time is used as the indicator of intensity, similar results are obtained –33% of the families received less than 6 hours of in-person case management time in their first year in the HFP, 18% of the families received over 24 hours, and 5% received over 50 hours.

Length of Case Management Contact. Of the 1298 HFP families tracked through the evaluation, 86% (1119) had exited the Program by April, 1995. The average amount of time in the Program was almost 14 months. Fifteen percent were in the Program less than 6 months, 38% from 6 months up to a year, and close to half (47%), a year or longer.

Among the families still in the Program by April 1995 (n = 179), the average Program tenure was 26 months. A few (7%) had been in the HFP for less than 1 year, having obtained housing right around the time the evaluation stopped tracking families. However, over half (52%) had been in the Program over 2 years and 17% had been in the HFP 3 years or more.

CROSS-SITE FINDINGS

The Homeless Families Program offered a general model of case management intervention that was implemented in various manners across the nine sites. Although statistical comparisons of the information based on the case manager survey and case manager time samples are not appropriate given the small number of case managers in most of the sites, it is possible to examine how the sites compare and contrast in their implementation of case management. The sites differ in the level of supervision offered; the number of case managers hired; and the intensity of the case management delivered. However, the site differences in how case management was delivered do not appear to be explained by case management configuration or other structural features. Of the four types of case manager configurations, only the resource coordinator/family advocate sites appear to share some characteristics in common and to differ from the majority of other sites.

Despite the differences noted, all nine sites have a number of features in common. Case managers in all sites work 1-1 with families, as opposed to working in teams or in other types of arrangements. Most sites provide some type of formal supervision, and most have almost all female case managers with background or experience in social work or psychology. In addition, the nature of the case manager contacts are remarkably similar. The most common family activities involved making regular visits to families, and arranging services and developing services plans.

Even in those aspects of case management where there is diversity across the sites, the sites still fall within upper and lower bounds on various aspects of the case management role that distinguish the HFP general model from other possible models of case management. For example, although there are considerable site differences in the daily time reportedly spent with families, only one site exceeded an average of 2 1/2 hours with families (approximately one-third of a case manager's day).

Overall case-load size represents a range, but average active case-loads are remarkably similar. Average contacts with families also represent a considerable range but, only in isolated incidents were families receiving multiple contacts a week. Finally, all sites were fairly consistent in providing long-term case management, having at least nearly a year of contact on average with families.

DISCUSSION AND IMPLICATIONS

The Homeless Families Program provides an unprecedented opportunity to examine the implementation of long-term case management for homeless families in multiple sites. When the model as implemented is compared to the intended framework, the most striking finding is that the delivery of case management was lower than what is typically expected from an "intensive case management" model. Although the typical case-load size was closer to what was expected (1:20) and the length of time families were involved in the Program was consistent with initial expectations, Program officials indicated that the number of visits and time spent with families were lower than they had originally anticipated. No one in the Program had set a specific expectation of contact, but there was some sense that weekly in-person contacts may be expected, at least early on, and that the case managers' role would be to interact intensively with the family, other service providers, and the broader system.

As the Program got underway and preliminary MIS data on case management intensity became available, explanations were developed as to why the intensity was lower than expected. A common explanation offered was that, because the Foundation had not explicitly paid for case management, the projects had less control over what they could expect from case managers leveraged from the system. HFP project directors could not always control how case managers from other agencies spent their time, whether they completed their paperwork, or the size and mix of their overall case-loads. Therefore, project case manager configuration was viewed as a key variable in explaining differences in case manager intensity.

However, not all site differences in the nature and amount of case management can be explained by project case management configuration. Although case managers in the project specific sites did not report having other social service responsibilities in their daily activities that stretched their time, case managers in four of the network sites and in the two resource coordinator/family advocate sites did report having other non-case management responsibilities. In these latter two projects, because they were small and advocacy-oriented, "leveraging" seemed to occur in the opposite direction, with HFP staff asked to fill other roles either in the agency or in the larger system. In addition, time on other activities that took time from families, such as travel, appeared to be explained by things other than case management configuration (such as geography, emphasis on home visits, etc.). Finally, case-load size was also expected to be higher in network sites where case managers had existing case-loads. In actuality, three of the sites that did not network but instead used case managers hired with HFP funds had among the highest case-loads.

A key insight gained from the analysis presented in this article is that even when the HFP projects were implemented as designed, the expected level of intensity could not be achieved. In the time sample, case managers spent, on average, about three quarters of their day engaged in such activities as paperwork, phone calls, meetings, office work, conferring with colleagues, travel and so on. Only one quarter of the day was thus used to meet face-to-face with families.[2] Clearly, it is impossible for case managers to spend all of their time directly with families. Yet, even if they could spend half of their day meeting with families, assuming a typical load of 20 families, this would result in an average of four hours a month (or one hour a week) in direct, face-to-face contact with each family. This suggests that the goal of spending one hour a week with a family represents the upper-limit for this model of case management. Typical activities such as conducting home visits, spending time in transit, and experiencing "no-shows" on the part of families serve to reduce the actual amount of time below this one-hour-a-week goal.

Furthermore, it is important to note that family needs may not always demand an intensive model of case management nor does available research indicate that more contact and time spent with families is related to greater effectiveness. In examining the relationship between family needs and intensity in this Program, no clear pattern has yet emerged across or within sites (see Rog et al., 1995a and 1995b). This is an area that will be explored more in future analyses.

The findings from this analysis suggest that developing models of practice for case managers need to go beyond determining case-load size and even optimal case mix. In particular, meeting families in their homes and assisting them in negotiating the system require time in transit that ultimately reduces the time they can spend with families. In addition, time needed for phone work with providers across the system, for necessary paperwork, for meeting both formally and informally with colleagues, and for typical office work all decrease the amount of time case managers can be expected to work with families. Although these activities support their work, they do reduce the time available for direct family contact. Likewise, if families' needs demand more of a case manager's time, it is likely that the case manager will have difficulties in getting necessary services, getting paperwork completed in a timely manner, and so on. Moreover, if a case manager is located within a broader organization that has demands for other non-case management related activities, the case manager is likely to be stretched in her responsibilities.

Therefore, to maintain balance, various strategies might be considered. For example, having teams of case managers to share responsibilities might offer creative arrangements for juggling key activities and maintaining an intensive level of direct client contact. Even partnerships with case management assistants who could accompany families to appointments, etc., could free up the case manager's time for arranging systems and developing services plans. In particular, developing peer supports with formerly homeless and now stable families who have successfully navigated the system might be a mechanism to consider, particularly in areas where families are housed in close proximity. In addition, an emphasis on training, standards, and supervision may help to keep case managers on course.

In the majority of HFP sites, case managers often came from existing agencies where they typically worked with families on a short-term basis, either while they were homeless or as they moved into housing. Most had not worked in families' homes nor did they have experience working with families over the long-term, negotiating with the system to meet emerging and changing needs of families. The transition from short-term case management to long-term models, at least in a few sites, necessitated the implementation of broad-based training, system supports, and the development of standards for case management delivery.

As other localities explore models for supporting formerly homeless families in the community, the HFP experience offers important lessons. Recognizing the other system and agency demands on the case managers, particularly if they are working in resource tight organizations, as well as the demands that are inherent in the role of the case manager, may provide insight into how best to support the case managers. Even the mere recognition of the many and often competing roles case managers are asked to fill may inform program developers of the need for expanding broader program supports. Case management has quickly become the "catch-all" for service intervention, particularly for populations that have varied and intense needs, yet a consistent operational definition continues to be elusive. The findings from this analysis provide a starting point for examining the integrity of the operational definition of intensive case management and suggest strategies for improving its delivery.

NOTES

1. A Section 8 certificate is a subsidy for housing such that a family pays 30% of its income toward rent and utilities. Unlike public housing, Section 8 housing is in the open-market; the certificate allows the family to seek a home from any landlord willing to participate in the Section 8 program by subsidizing that portion of the rent and utilities that exceed 30% of the family's income.

2. The "Yesterday" interview is likely to underestimate less frequent activities, such as meetings, trainings, paperwork and so on. Future analyses will examine case management activities occurring over longer periods of time.

REFERENCES

Center for Mental Health Services. (1994). *Making a difference: Interim status report of the McKinney demonstration program for homeless adults with serious mental illness* (DHHS Publication No. SMA94-3014). Washington, DC: U.S. Government Printing Office.

Friedmutter, C. (1989). *Services-enriched housing for homeless families.* Prepared for The Robert Wood Johnson Foundation, Princeton, New Jersey.

Helvie, C. and Alexy, B. (1992). Using after-shelter case management to improve outcomes for families with children. *Public Health Reports, 107*(5), 585-588.

MDS Associates. (1993, February). *Case management for special populations: Practitioner perspectives and recommendations* (HRSA Contract No. 240-91-0066). Prepared for the Department of Health and Human Services, Health Resources and Services Administration, Bureau of Primary Care–Division of Programs for Special Populations.

Rife, J., First, R., Greenlee, R., Miller, L., and Feichter, M. (1991). Case management with homeless mentally ill people. *Health and Social Work, 16*(1), 58-67.

Rog, D., Hambrick, R., Holupka, C., McCombs, K., Gilbert, A., and Brito, M. (1994). *The Homeless Families Program: Interim Benchmarks.* Prepared for The Robert Wood Johnson Foundation, Princeton, New Jersey.

Rog, D., Holupka, C., and McCombs-Thornton, K. (1995a). Implementation of the Homeless Families Program: 1. Service models, and preliminary outcomes. *American Journal of Orthopsychiatry, 65*(4), 502-513.

Rog, D., McCombs-Thornton, K., Gilbert-Mongelli, A., Brito, M., and Holupka, C. (1995b). Implementation of the Homeless Families Program: 2. Characteristics, strengths, and needs of participant families. *American Journal of Orthopsychiatry, 65*(4), 514-528.

Rossi, P. (1994). Troubling families: Family homelessness in America. *American Behavioral Scientist, 37*(3), 342-395.

Weitzman, B., and Berry, C. (1994). *Formerly homeless families and the transition to permanent housing: High-risk families and the role of intensive case management services.* New York: New York University, The Health Research Program, Robert F. Wagner Graduate School of Public Service.

Matching the Needs of the Homeless with Those of the Disabled: Empowerment Through Caregiving

Joseph R. Ferrari
DePaul University

William Billows
University of Toledo

Leonard A. Jason
DePaul University

Gregory J. Grill
Needs Foundation

SUMMARY. Previously homeless women (17) and men (12) were surveyed on their experience as a caregiver to physically challenged senior citizen clients (16 men, 13 women: age $M = 64.7$, $SD = 16.8$). Caregivers had training in service delivery and experience before the survey. More satisfaction than stress from providing care was reported by caregivers. Caregiving satisfaction was significantly positively related to global life satisfaction and a sense of personal vulnerability to being disabled. Caregiving stress was significantly negatively related to perceived knowledge of the disability. Overall, these previously homeless caregivers reported that providing care to the disabled was positive, and would be repeated and recommended to others. *[Article copies available for a fee from The Haworth Document Delivery Service: 1-800-342-9678. E-mail address: getinfo@haworth.com]*

[Haworth co-indexing entry note]: "Matching the Needs of the Homeless with Those of the Disabled: Empowerment Through Caregiving." Ferrari, Joseph R. et al. Co-published simultaneously in *Journal of Prevention & Intervention in the Community* (The Haworth Press, Inc.) Vol. 15, No. 2, 1997, pp. 83-92; and: *Diversity Within the Homeless Population: Implications for Intervention* (ed: Elizabeth M. Smith, and Joseph R. Ferrari) The Haworth Press, Inc., 1997, pp. 83-92. Single or multiple copies of this article are available for a fee from The Haworth Document Delivery Service [1-800-342-9678, 9:00 a.m. - 5:00 p.m. (EST). E-mail address: getinfo@haworth.com].

The vast majority of "caregiver burnout" research has been on health care providers (e.g., Maslach & Jackson, 1986; Epstein & Silvern, 1990; Vanyperen, Buunk, & Schaufeli, 1992). Individuals in the health care profession have high task demands when servicing the ill, and at extremes these pressures may result in impaired performance and poor judgements (see Russo, 1993). Human service individuals who do 'people work' of some kind may experience high levels of exhaustion or stress (both psychological and physical), cynicism, and negativism (Maslach & Jackson, 1986; Zastrow, 1984). Based on extensive research, Maslach and Jackson (1986) identified three factors as components to high levels of stress from caregiving, namely: (a) *Emotional Exhaustion* (EE), the feeling of being overextended and exhausted; (b) *Personal Accomplishment* (PA), feelings of competence and successful achievement in one's work with people, with low levels of PA resulting in stress; and, (c) *Depersonalization,* an unfeeling and impersonal response towards recipients of one's service, care, treatment, or instruction.

In the present study, we examined self-reported levels of stress (perhaps, in the form of EE), and personal satisfaction (a possible index of PA), among an atypical target population of care providers–homeless men and women. Homelessness continues to be a problem of great social significance in North America, both by professionals and by the general public (Breakey & Fischer, 1990; Toro & McDonell, 1992). There are increasing reports of the prevalence of personal adjustment problems experienced by the homeless, including such disorders as depression, alcoholism, and schizophrenia (Fischer & Breakey, 1991; Toro & Wall, 1991). In fact, the available data indicate that homeless women, relative to homeless men, report higher levels of psychological distress (see Maurin, Russell, & Memmott, 1989; Ritchey, LaGory, & Mullis, 1991). Consequently, innovative programs that provide homeless persons with employable skills and, in turn, that improves their self-concept seem worthy of investigation.

The "Needs Foundation," located in Chicago, IL, was developed to empower the homeless with employment skills that facilitated their sense of personal development. This non-profit organization trained economically disadvantaged homeless individuals to function and retain employment plus housing with disabled persons by matching such persons with chronic disabled persons from the community. Homeless men and women were then trained as in-home, non-medical care providers ("personal assistants"). This program responded to the needs, services, and empowerment of the poor by developing a program which gave the homeless skills to take better care of themselves, to improve their job skills and life options, and to make available housing options through employment opportunities. Many clients required care 24 hours a day, 5 days per week. The caregiver received a 12-month series of inservice workshops through the Foundation that included how to provide daily maintenance care (e.g., cooking, light cleaning, shopping) and companionship. Specific workshops were tailored to careproviders' skills. The disabled, elderly client paid the personal assistant a set weekly rate (determined by the number of days worked) and provided housing arrangements. In short, caregivers acted as "buddies" to their client, providing non-medical care that ranged from companionship to daily maintenance care.

To measure caregiver satisfaction and stress among the homeless men and women, the present study used the *Caregiver Scale* developed by Ferrari, McCown, and Pantano (1993). These authors administered this scale to 251 healthcare workers from Philadelphia and 91 volunteer "buddies" from upstate New York who cared for persons with AIDS (PWAs). Buddies offered non-medical care (e.g., light housework, some cooking, occasional drives to services) and companionship. After six months, healthcare providers reported increased stress and depression from their work with PWAs. The buddies, however, reported that the greater their satisfaction from caring for PWAs the more positive their attitude toward PWAs, and the less prejudice and social discrimination toward PWAs they held. Ferrari, Jason, and Salina (1995) used this scale with members of religious communities in New York City who volunteered pastoral care to PWAs. Satisfaction from providing care was related to pastoral training, an understanding of the spiritual nature of death, and a positive attitude toward PWAs, while stress was inversely related to pastoral training to deal with death. The pastoral volunteers reported greater satisfaction and lower stress from caregiving to PWAs than the volunteer buddies cited in Ferrari et al. (1993). With each sample (health care workers, buddies, clergy), no significant gender difference on the caregiver scale was obtained. In the present study, the validity of this scale was extended to another target population of caregivers (homeless men and women) and to a population of chronically disabled senior citizens who were not terminally ill (such as from AIDS).

In addition, the present study included a measure of global life satisfaction. Life satisfaction reflected how well a person integrated and weighted different domains in life to produce an overall sense of subjective well-being (see Pavot & Diener, 1993). The use of this scale was to ascertain whether former homeless individuals who had gone through a service care training program and now were acting as careproviders reported overall contentment with their life. Also, participants completed a measure of their attitudes as careproviders to physically challenged persons. While studies typically examined the general population's attitude toward the physically challenged (see Dunn, 1994), few studies explored the caregiver's perspective of the physically challenged–those persons the careprovider serves directly. This scale was included in the present study to determine how caregivers of chronically ill persons perceived the nature of their client's disability. No apriori predictions were made concerning this scale given the exploratory nature of the project.

Thus, this exploratory study was an evaluation of formerly homeless caregivers and their clients in a unique rehabilitation-like program located in a metropolitan area (Chicago, IL). The study focused on the caregivers' self-reported levels of stress and satisfaction from providing care, global sense of personal life satisfaction, and attitudes toward disabled persons. Although brief in measures and employing a small sample size, this study may shed light on the utility of an innovative program to assist homeless men and women.

METHOD

Participants, Clients, and Agency Purpose/Training Description

There were 17 women and 12 men (age $M = 45.18$ years old; $SD = 12.92$) trained through the "Needs Foundation" program as non-medical "caregivers." Most caregivers were Caucasian (58.60%), and had either a high school/GED degree (27.60%) or some college experience (27.60%). On average, they had spent 3.72 months ($SD = 3.94$) homeless prior to involvement in this program. None of these caregivers were diagnosed with psychiatric disorders at the time of this study. Medical and psychological histories of the caregivers were not available in order to maintain confidentiality and anonymity. Caregivers also reported spending an average of 13.86 months ($SD = 11.01$) with the Needs Foundation. At the time of this study, caregivers were providers to at least one other client ($M = 1.04$, $SD = 1.23$) and spent 8.75 months ($SD = 8.24$) with their current client. Caregivers received room, board, and a stipend of $100.00 for a five day work week, and $150.00 for a seven day work week.

There were 16 men and 13 women included who were disabled clients. Their mean age was 64.71 years old ($SD = 16.81$), and most were Caucasian (75.90%). These disabled clients were physically as opposed to cognitively challenged, with difficulties in gross motor movement problems. In order to maintain confidentiality about the clients, no further demographic information was collected on the clients.

The Needs Foundation placed an ad in local newspapers designed for homeless individuals requesting that interested persons contact the agency. Members of the Foundation also networked with area shelters, and every shelter was sent information about the program. Individuals who responded to the ad were asked to make an appointment with a staff member to come to the office to be screened. Those individuals who came to the office were given a criminal background check, and personal and employment references were contacted. Also, medical and skill level evaluations were performed. Potential caregivers were reimbursed by the agency for the transportation costs of these screening components.

Because the goal of the agency was to reach, screen, train, and place as many qualified homeless people into the program, caregivers were provided a training program. A training program with a local rehabilitation center to assist with educating caregivers on being live-in assistants was developed. Training began with a one-day, eight hour course that covered proper nutrition, hygiene, wheelchair safety, bathing, communication skills, and how to keep a schedule. Caregivers had to go through this program before being placed with a client. Other workshops were arranged during the year as issues and training needs arose. Medical treatment was handled by a registered nurse.

Psychometric Scales

Participants completed Ferrari et al.'s (1993) *Caregiver Scale*. This 14-item, 7-point (1 = low; 7 = high) self-report inventory assessed the emotional experiences from working with chronically ill individuals, such as persons with AIDS (PWAs). Subscales included a personal *satisfaction* subscale (*CSAT,* 7 items: e.g., "Working with [an elderly-disabled] persons is adding meaning to my life") and an emotional *stress* subscale (*CSTR,* 7 items: e.g., "Helping someone with [a disability] has burned me out"). In the present study, references to PWAs and AIDS were substituted with "persons with disabilities," in order to demonstrate the adaptability of the scale to a different target population. Ferrari et al. (1993) reported the satisfaction and stress scales are negatively related ($-.68$), internally consistent ($r = .82$ and $.80$, respectively), and temporally stable (6 month $r = .68$ and $.72$, respectively) with AIDS caregivers. Stress scores were related to depression after six months working with PWAs, and both stress and satisfaction scores have not been related to social desirability scores. This caregiver scale have been validated with health care workers, volunteer "buddies" of PWAs, and pastoral caregivers (Ferrari et al., 1993; 1995).

In addition, caregivers completed Diener, Emmons, Larsen, and Griffin's (1985) uni-dimensional *Satisfaction with Life Scale (LSAT)*, a global measure of the cognitive-judgmental aspects of a person's life. Life satisfaction is a judgement of how satisfied people are with their present state of affairs when evaluating their subjective well-being, thereby centering on a person's own judgments and not those imposed by external forces (Diener, 1984). The LSAT is a 5 item, 7-point rating scale (1 = strongly disagree; 7 = strongly agree) with questions including "In most ways, my life is close to my ideal." and "I am satisfied with my life." Diener et al. (1985) reported that the LSAT has acceptable internal consistency ($r =$ .89), retest reliability ($r = .82$), and good construct and predicitive validities for a research tool (see also Pavot & Diener, 1993).

Also, participants completed the 20 item, 5-point *Interaction with Disabled Persons Scale* (IDP), developed by Gething (1994). The IDP measures discomfort based on actual social interactions with people with disabilities. Previous factor analysis by the scale's developer indicated that five subscales explained 57.9% of the common variance, of which three were examined in the current study. These three subscales included *discomfort in social interaction* (6 items: e.g., "I feel uncomfortable and find it hard to relax" and "I feel unsure because I don't know how to behave") that related to behaviors and reactions on meeting someone with a disability, *perceived level of information* (5 items: e.g., "I feel ignorant about disabled people" and "I am aware of the problems disabled people face") that asks about a person's knowledge about a disability, and *vulnerability* (4 items: e.g., "I am grateful I do not have such a burden" and "Contact with a disabled person reminds me of my own vulnerability") where a person may believe they are susceptible to the disability and/or are grateful that they do not have the disability. The scale's total scale score has acceptable reliability (.79), and was inversely related to distress over associations with the disabled, overall rejection of people with disabilities, and rejection of intimate relationships with the disabled (Gething, 1994).

Procedures

Caregivers were sent through the mail a consent form, demographic sheet, and the three psychometric scales. Participants were assured confidentiality of results, with the consent form to be returned directly to an administrative office at the Needs Foundation and the set of measures returned separately to the first author. All but one of the 30 careproviders involved in the Needs Foundation program at the time of the study returned the completed questionnaires within six weeks of initial mailing.

RESULTS AND DISCUSSION

Profile of Caregivers

Chi square comparisons were performed between these formerly homeless men and women on self-reported characteristics. There was no significant gender difference on previous residential experience, types of prior co-habitants, reasons for terminating prior caregiving relationships, immediate life goals, and personal strivings beyond the Needs Foundation program. Many participants (41.4%) entered the Needs Foundation project from a homeless shelter, and had lived either alone (27.6%) or with a non-relative (27.6%). Most participants (55.2%) did not respond to why they left a previous caregiving position within the Foundation. In terms of immediate goals, however, participants typically reported they desired to continue helping others (27.6%) or live independently (27.6%), and many (48.3%) claimed they would like to continue as a caregiver with the Needs Foundation or some other similar agency. In fact, all participants (100%) stated they would recommend the Needs Foundation to other homeless persons.

It seems that those men and women who were involved as caregivers to the disabled were persons who came from homeless shelters, lived separately from relatives, and had previous experience as a caregiver. Furthermore, these caregivers enjoyed providing care to disabled senior citizens. The goal of the Needs Foundation to create livable, meaningful living situations for homeless persons seemed to have occurred. Caregivers did report that they eventually wanted to live independently, but they also desired to continue with the Needs Foundation program or a similar care-providing project.

Analyses of Self-Reported Psychometric Measures

A zero-order correlation matrix between self-reported psychometric measures also was performed. Table 1 shows the mean (standard deviation), coefficient alpha, and correlation coefficients on these measures. It appears that most scales had acceptable alpha coefficients, except the PLI and VUL subscales. Perhaps, for these scales the small sample size of 29 respondents and the fact that both subscales included only 4 or 5 items reduced the amount of variability between items. It also must be noted that the small sample size in this study may have affected the level of statistical significance in much of these analyses. The probability of obtaining significant relationships with only 29 respondents is low; consequently, marginally significant relationships (at the $p < .06$ level, for example) were reported.

TABLE 1. Mean Score, Alpha, and Bivariate Correlate Between Self-Reported Psychometric Measures

	M	CSAT	CSTR	LSAT	DSI	PLI	VUL
CAREGIVING:							
satisfaction	38.72	[.76]					
(CSAT)	(5.24)						
stress	16.07	−.331*	[.74]				
(CSTR)	(5.36)						
LIFE SATISFACTION	16.66	.349*	−.078	[.86]			
(LSAT):	(6.59)						
INTERACTION WITH DISABLED PERSONS							
discomfort in social	10.83	−.332*	.253	.050	[.75]		
interaction (DSI)	(2.69)						
perceived level of	11.79	−.063	−.360**	.199	.312	[.54]	
information (PLI)	(2.23)						
vulnerability	13.31	.739**	−.081	.206	−.139	.266	[.62]
(VUL)	(2.52)						

n = 29   *p < .06   **p < .01

Note. Standard deviations are in parentheses, and coefficient alpha is in brackets.

Still, an interesting inter-correlation matrix from scores on these scales emerged with the present sample. Satisfaction was inversely related to stress from being a careprovider to the elderly, even when controlling for global life satisfaction (partial $r = -.300, p < .06$. Moreover, participants reported significantly more satisfaction than stress as a caregiver, $t (27) = 14.20, p < .001$. Consistent with other studies using this "Caregiver Scale" (Ferrari et al., 1993; 1995), caregiver satisfaction and stress seemed to be relatively independent constructs, and providers perceive more "pleasure than pain" from the experience.

Caregiver satisfaction also was related both positively to global life satisfaction and negatively to discomfort in social interactions with disabled elderly. In addition, caregiver satisfaction was positively related to a sense of vulnerability to the physical disability. In other words, these former homeless men and women claimed that the more satisfied they were from providing care to elderly disabled persons the more overall satisfied they were with their life, and the more caregiver satisfaction they experienced the less disfavorably they were toward interacting with these elderly disabled persons.

Of course, much of these analyses were correlational, so the direction of these relationships cannot be determined. Furthermore, no measure of social desirability was taken with the present participants so it is not possible to ascertain whether responses to any measure was a function of response biases. No initial assessments at entry to the program as baseline rates for change were taken. Nevertheless, it seems these former homeless men and women found their experience with the Needs Foundation to be pleasant. Providing care for disabled elderly was a meaningful, satisfying experience in the lives of these men and women. The training and employment these individuals received may have supplied hope and optimism to persons with few options.

From a societal and public health perspective, the results of the present study suggest that programs such as the Needs Foundations deserve closer examination. To the extent that participants report overall satisfaction instead of stress as a caregiver, then this program may be a cost effective way of addressing homelessness in many communities. Homeless individuals are provided important service skills and, similar to an internship, these men and women receive on-the-job experience. Ultimately, the careproviders desired independent living from a program such as the Needs Foundation. These careproviders did report that they would like to continue in the future as non-medical careproviders. Thus, it seems that programs such as the Needs Foundations may hold promise and potential for dealing with the issue of "retooling" homeless individuals with skills that may make them competitive as employees.

Further research is needed to ascertain the careprovider's desire to appear socially "correct" in regards to their work with the Needs Foundation. Baseline and repeated measures are needed to plot changes (if any) as participants continue through the training and employment within the program. Greater detail on both the caregivers and their clients also is warranted. Based on the current study, it is not known how successful this program would be in other urban, and even rural, communities thereby limiting its generalizability. Also, data must be collected on the recipients of care (here, the elderly disabled) to determine their satisfaction and stress from involvement in the program. Still, this brief, exploratory study offers a description and initial assessment of a seemingly successful program to empower homeless men and women.

REFERENCES

Diener, E., Emmons, R.A., Larsen, R.J., & Griffin, S. (1985). The Satisfaction with Life Scale. *Journal of Personality Assessment, 49,* 71-75.

Diener, E. (1984). Subjective well-being. *Psychological Bulletin, 95,* 542-575.

Dunn, D.S. (Ed.). (1994). Psychosocial perspectives on disability [special issue]. *Journal of Social Behavior and Personality.*

Epstein, S.R., & Silvern, L.E. (1990). Staff burnout in shelters for battered women: A challenge for the 90's. *Response, 13,* 9-12.

Ferrari, J.R., McCown, W., & Pantano, J. (1993). Experiencing satisfaction and stress as an AIDS care provider: The (AIDS) Caregiver Scale. *Evaluation and the Health Professions, 16,* 295-310.

Ferrari, J.R., Jason, L.A., & Salina, D. (1995). Pastoral care and AIDS: Assessing the stress and satisfaction from caring for persons with AIDS. *Pastoral Psychology, 44,* 99-110.

Fischer, P.J., & Breakey, W.R. (1991). The epidemiology of alcohol, drug, and mental disorders among homeless persons. *American Psychologist, 46,* 1115-1128.

Gething, L. (1994). The Interaction with Disabled Persons Scale. *Journal of Social Behavior and Personality, 9,* 23-42.

Maslach, C., & Jackson, S.E. (1986). *Maslach burnout inventory* (2nd ed.) Palo Alto, CA: Consulting Psychologist Press.

Maurin, J.T., Russell, L., & Memmott, R.J. (1989). An exploration of gender differences among the homeless. *Research in Nursing and Health, 12,* 315-321.

Pavot, W., & Diener, E. (1993). Review of the Satisfaction with Life Scale. *Psychological Assessment, 5,* 164-172.

Ritchey, F.J., LaGory, M., & Mullis, J. (1991). Gender differences in health risks and physical symptoms among the homeless. *Journal of Health and Social Behavior, 32,* 33-48.

Russo, J.R. (1993). *Serving and surviving as a human-service worker.* Prospect Heights, IL: Waveland Press.

Toro, P.A., & Wall, D.D. (1991). Research on homeless persons: Diagnostic comparisons and practice implications. *Professional Psychology: Research and Practice, 22,* 479-488.

Vanyperen, N., Buunk, B., & Schaufeli, W. (1992). Communal orientation and the burnout syndrome among nurses. *Journal of Applied Social Psychology, 22,* 173-189.

Zastrow, C. (1984). Understanding and preventing burnout. *British Journal of Social Work, 14,* 141-155.

Index

Page number followed by a t indicates table.

93

Haworth
DOCUMENT DELIVERY
SERVICE

This valuable service provides a single-article order form for any article from a Haworth journal.

- *Time Saving:* No running around from library to library to find a specific article.
- *Cost Effective:* All costs are kept down to a minimum.
- *Fast Delivery:* Choose from several options, including same-day FAX.
- *No Copyright Hassles:* You will be supplied by the original publisher.
- *Easy Payment:* Choose from several easy payment methods.

Open Accounts Welcome for ...
- Library Interlibrary Loan Departments
- Library Network/Consortia Wishing to Provide Single-Article Services
- Indexing/Abstracting Services with Single Article Provision Services
- Document Provision Brokers and Freelance Information Service Providers

---

MAIL or *FAX* THIS ENTIRE ORDER FORM TO:

Haworth Document Delivery Service
The Haworth Press, Inc.
10 Alice Street
Binghamton, NY 13904-1580

or FAX: 1-800-895-0582
or CALL: 1-800-342-9678
9am-5pm EST

PLEASE SEND ME PHOTOCOPIES OF THE FOLLOWING SINGLE ARTICLES:
1) Journal Title: _____
   Vol/Issue/Year: _____ Starting & Ending Pages: _____
Article Title: _____
_____

2) Journal Title: _____
   Vol/Issue/Year: _____ Starting & Ending Pages: _____
Article Title: _____
_____

3) Journal Title: _____
   Vol/Issue/Year: _____ Starting & Ending Pages: _____
Article Title: _____
_____

4) Journal Title: _____
   Vol/Issue/Year: _____ Starting & Ending Pages: _____
Article Title: _____
_____

(See other side for Costs and Payment Information)

COSTS: Please figure your cost to order quality copies of an article.

1. Set-up charge per article: $8.00
   ($8.00 × number of separate articles) _____
2. Photocopying charge for each article:

    1-10 pages: $1.00 _____

    11-19 pages: $3.00 _____

    20-29 pages: $5.00 _____

    30+ pages: $2.00/10 pages _____

3. Flexicover (optional): $2.00/article _____
4. Postage & Handling: US: $1.00 for the first article/
    $.50 each additional article _____

    Federal Express: $25.00 _____

    Outside US: $2.00 for first article/
    $.50 each additional article _____

5. Same-day FAX service: $.35 per page _____

GRAND TOTAL: _____

METHOD OF PAYMENT: (please check one)

❑ Check enclosed   ❑ Please ship and bill. PO # _____
(sorry we can ship and bill to bookstores only! All others must pre-pay)

❑ Charge to my credit card: ❑ Visa; ❑ MasterCard; ❑ Discover;
                             ❑ American Express;

Account Number: _____ Expiration date: _____

Signature: ✗ _____

Name: _____ Institution: _____

Address: _____

_____

City: _____ State: _____ Zip: _____

Phone Number: _____ FAX Number: _____

MAIL or *FAX* THIS ENTIRE ORDER FORM TO:

Haworth Document Delivery Service
The Haworth Press, Inc.
10 Alice Street
Binghamton, NY 13904-1580

or FAX: 1-800-895-0582
or CALL: 1-800-342-9678
      9am-5pm EST)

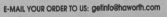